SALTWATER
FISHING

IN SOUTH AFRICA

SALTWATER
FISHING

IN SOUTH AFRICA

HENNIE CROUS

Struik Publishers
(a division of New Holland Publishing (South Africa) (Pty) Ltd)
Cornelis Struik House
80 McKenzie Street
Cape Town, 8001

New Holland Publishing is a member of the Johnnic Publishing Group.
www.struik.co.za
Log on to our photographic website **www.imagesofafrica.co.za**
for an African experience.

First published 1994
Second edition 2000

10 9 8 7 6 5 4 3 2

Front cover photos: C. Norman (top, bottom right, bottom centre right,
bottom centre left); *Getaway* – D. Rogers (bottom left)

Edited by Tracey Hawthorne and Valerie Streak
Designed by René Greef and Lyndall Hamilton
Cover designed by Janice Evans
Typeset by Lyndall Hamilton

Reproduction by Hirt & Carter Cape (Pty) Ltd
Printed and bound by CTP Book Printers

ISBN 1 86872 307 0

CONTENTS

ACKNOWLEDGEMENTS

Although I have been associated with the sea and fishing virtually all my life, assembling the information for this book has not been easy, and in the process I have had to draw on the knowledge and experience of many of my angling friends around the country. I therefore wish to thank most warmly the following people:

Simon Walker, with whom I have spent many a day fishing from the rocks; Dave Goodman – a mine of information on shore and boat angling; Nic de Kock, a purist as far as tackle and tackle preparation are concerned and one of the best all-round anglers; deep-sea fishing companion, Brian Cohen; brother-in-law Harold Webster, who taught me how to fish for bronze bream; fellow-angler, Rob Naysmith, who in particular provided information about 'couta fishing in KwaZulu-Natal; Simon Chater of the Oceanographic Research Institute for photographs of KwaZulu-Natal angling, and for his valuable comments and information; Pierre Malan and fellow ski-boat fisherman Tony Bradfield, for the loan of photographs; Tinker Lures and Fred Tucker Agencies for the loan of all lures, tackle, equipment and protective clothing for photographic purposes; and my son, Gavin, and his friend, Bruce Wilsnach, who ably assisted with the 'field' photographic sessions.

In respect of the formal production of the first edition of this book, my gratitude goes to Tony van Dalsen, for his meticulous illustrations; Charles Didcott for his excellent photography and patient persistence in waiting for the 'right moment'; Rudy van der Elst for the use of his species photographs and also for going out of his way to take additional photographs to meet specific needs; Sean Lange for valuable information relating to KwaZulu-Natal species and angling; and Struik Publishers for their publishing expertise – in particular, Valerie Streak and Lyndall Hamilton for going much more than the extra mile.

Finally, I would like to pay tribute to my friend, John Schoeman, for his motivation, support and interest throughout the writing of this project, and of course to my wife, Marge, and daughter, Janice, for their enthusiastic encouragement at all times – and for just being there.

PREFACE

So often after a day's fishing, when one angler has been particularly successful while others in the party have struggled to catch anything, the inevitable post-mortem will bring to light subtle differences in tackle and rigging or bait presentation. And time and again it will be found that the consistently success-ful angler is the one who is aware that changes in the prevailing conditions can affect the behaviour and feeding habits of fish, and who instinctively adapts his fishing technique accordingly.

In writing this book my objective has been to provide a useful guide to salt-water fishing – principally for newcomers to the sport but I hope that much will be of interest to those who have been fishing for some time. I make no claim to have written a comprehensive manual, but, over the years, in introducing people of all ages to angling, and assisting others to aquire the skills necessary to make successful angling much more than a matter of luck, I have found the better the foundation a beginner has, the better angler he becomes. This foundation is what I hope the novice will gain from this book.

In conclusion I wish to draw the reader's attention to the vital need to con-serve our fishing resource and its environment. Easier access to fishing spots, four-wheel-drive vehicles and simply an increase in the number of anglers is putting severe pressure on our shores and marine life. In the interests of all, I appeal to our anglers to treat our marine resources and shores with respect. Observe the catch restrictions and join the tag-and-release programme, details of which are outlined at the back of this book, and take great care not to desecrate our beautiful shores. If everyone adopts a responsible attitude, fishing will remain the relaxing and rewarding pastime it has always been and - its future will be guaranteed for the generations who follow.

Hennie Crous
May 1993

CHAPTER ONE

THE INFLUENCE
OF NATURE

'Old anglers – old not necessarily in years but in practice – show consistently good results, envied by their less experienced fellows. To acquire such skill one must have the talent for constructiveness and cultivate it by observing the water conditions in which successful rodmen vary their style of tackle. The careful study of weather and the condition of the water are the real key to successful sea angling.'

So said an acknowledged authority on Cape fish species, C. Leo Biden, in his book *Sea Angling Fishes of the Cape*, first published in 1930. Indeed, there are certain anglers who consistently catch more fish than the anglers around them. Is this luck, or are they doing something the average angler does not know of or has not thought about?

Beach angling is at its best early in the morning or at sunset.

Fishermen today are fond of saying how easy it was in the 'old' days to make consistently good catches and how different things are today. There may have been more fish and there was certainly less angler pressure on the resource then, but the factors influencing the behaviour of fish are many and liable to change from day to day. The successful angler is the one who, above all, is aware of these conditions and has developed the ability to watch and evaluate them and to go fishing only when he feels that, according to his experience, they are all favourable.

Being aware of all the factors in nature that may influence fishing conditions and using them to decide when and where to go will help you in finding just the right spot from which to cast your line. If you ensure that you fish at a place where all the conditions are right – where the colour of the water, the temperature and the size of the swell have been taken into consideration – then the success of your trip will depend largely on your fishing skills.

The successful angler with a fine specimen of kob.

So, once you become aware of how the weather and the state of the sea may influence your catch rate and start applying this knowledge, things can improve!

There are a number of natural systems, such as currents, upwelling, tides, temperature and salinity, which may influence the behaviour of fish, play a major role in the distribution of their young, or influence their supply of food or where they shelter. There are times of the year when conditions may be at an optimum for any one species, and a change in any one of the natural systems may cause a shift in the location of such optimum conditions. Getting to know these systems will ultimately improve your chances of being at the right fishing spot at the right time.

OCEAN CURRENTS

The warm Agulhas current, flowing down the east coast of Africa in a southerly direction, has its origin in the more northerly South Equatorial current. The Agulhas current transports tropical water from the KwaZulu-Natal coast and carries the eggs and larvae of fish species, such as shad (elf), to the sandy-beach areas of Cape Agulhas and beyond to the food-rich bays of the southwestern Cape coast. This is where the juveniles feed and grow.

During the winter months mature fish use the inshore counter-current to migrate back to the coastal waters of KwaZulu-Natal to spawn, and in so doing complete the cycle. This counter-current probably plays an important role in the famous 'sardine run' along the south coast of KwaZulu-Natal during the winter months.

According to oceanographers, the average speed of the Agulhas current is between 1 and 2 metres per second, and some 60 million cubic metres of water are transported each second. (This translates to between 4 and 7 kilometres per hour and has been recorded at speeds as great as 12 kilometres per hour.) The current flows fast where the continental shelf is narrow but in areas such as Cape Agulhas, where the shelf width is 100 nautical miles (approximately 200 kilometres), the current spreads out and provides warm water and optimum fishing conditions during the summer months.

The Benguela current transports the nutrient-rich cool Antarctic water up the west coast of Africa in a northerly direction and carries with it the eggs and larvae of pelagic fish, such as anchovy and sardine (pilchard), which spawn in the vicinity of the Agulhas Bank during the spring and summer months. Juvenile pelagic fish migrate shorewards and then commence their return journey to the Agulhas Bank close inshore, past places such as Hondeklip Bay, Lambert's Bay and St Helena Bay, growing rapidly while feeding in the cool plankton-rich waters off the west coast. These large shoals of anchovies and sardines are the primary food source of predatory fish such as the Cape snoek, yellowtail, kob, geelbek and tuna.

UPWELLING

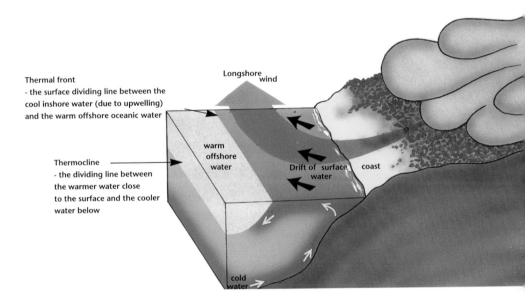

Thermal front
- the surface dividing line between the cool inshore water (due to upwelling) and the warm offshore oceanic water

Thermocline
- the dividing line between the warmer water close to the surface and the cooler water below

Longshore wind

warm offshore water

Drift of surface water

coast

cold water

Upwelling is the process whereby cool, nutrient-rich water is brought to the surface; and it is the combination of sunlight and carbon dioxide with the nutrient salts dissolved in the surface water that promotes the growth of microscopic plants (phytoplankton) through the process of photosynthesis. This is the first link in the sea food-chain.

How upwelling takes place.

An upwelling causes the temperature of inshore waters to drop and frequently creates very clear conditions, which are unfavourable for the inshore angler. Close inshore near headlands such as Cape Recife, Cape St Francis, Cape St Blaize, Cape Agulhas and Cape Point, coastal upwelling

occurs when easterly winds blow parallel to the coast. In the southern hemisphere, because of the earth's rotation, the effect of this wind is to blow surface water to the left, offshore; the easterly or southeasterly winds that blow during the summer months, therefore, cause the surface water to move away from the shore. Cold water then rises to replace the water being transported offshore.

This phenomenon, with its attendant ice-blue, clear water, is typically seen along the western coast of the Cape Peninsula when a gale-force southeaster, the 'Cape doctor', has been blowing for a few days.

The cooler coastal water is separated from the warm offshore water by a front. The offshore tuna fishermen of the south-western Cape are familiar with this front, which they invariably encounter some 15 or even 20 nautical miles offshore. This thermal front is a very dynamic area and, with the presence of baitfish such as anchovy, sardine (pilchard) or redeye being present, is a favourite feeding spot for yellowfin tuna.

TEMPERATURE

The successful angler – whether fishing from the shore, close inshore from a boat or some distance offshore on the gamefish grounds – is aware of the value of knowing the temperature of the water in which his target species prefers to feed, and by continuously monitoring the temperature he will eventually develop a 'feel' for the correct conditions in which to fish.

Fish are cold-blooded animals and changes in temperature affect their feeding habits and swimming speed, as well as longer-term factors such as growth and reproduction. (Fish may undertake long migrations to spawn in an area where the temperatures are suitable, to ensure the survival of their young.)

Anglers sometimes plan a fishing trip weeks ahead without taking into consideration any possible changes in the weather, wind direction and, as a result, temperature. Consequently they may end up fishing where the conditions are totally unsuitable. Keeping a careful watch on weather conditions, and knowing how any change may influence the surface temperature of the sea at your favourite fishing spots, will help you decide where best to go. The experienced angler keeps this kind of information in mind when weighing up when or where to go fishing.

The shore fisherman can measure the temperature of the water by simply holding a thermometer, obtainable from a chemist, in the water or in a container of water. The boat fisherman has the option of fitting a temperature gauge or purchasing a video-type echosounder which, as part of the normal display, indicates the sea surface temperature as well as the speed of the vessel.

Opposite above: The same wind blowing across a headland or peninsula can create ideal fishing conditions when it blows onshore (left) or conditions at their worst when it blows offshore (right).
Opposite below: *Migrating bait shoals that occur in the nutrient-rich coastal waters attract predatory species such as the snoek.*
Below: *Shoaling species such as kob are particularly sensitive to changes in temperature.*

TIDES

Tides are an important factor and influence the fishing environment twice each day: reefs are covered and uncovered, the water depth is forever changing, and floating bits and pieces of food as well as shoals of baitfish are transported by the ebb and flow.

In every four-week month there are two neap tides and two spring tides. Neap tides occur when the moon has completed its first and third quarters and the gravitational pull of the sun and the moon oppose each other, resulting in a minimum of tidal movement. During spring tides, when the sun, moon and earth are close to being in line with one another (that is, when the moon is in its new and full stages) and the gravitational pull of the sun and the moon are in harmony, there is a maximum tidal movement resulting in very high and very low tides.

Most of the fish species that occur in the intertidal zone (such as galjoen, dassie or blacktail and bronze bream) feed best on an incoming tide, and good catches can be made at spring tide, when the water rushes in, swirling into gullies and disturbing piles of rotting weed, or covering mussel-encrusted reefs with enough water to allow these agile swimmers to feed. A successful shore-fishing trip should therefore be planned with the phase of the moon as well as the state of the tide in mind. However, as the moon rises some 50 minutes later each day, determining the time of a tide is no simple matter. A tide table is therefore an essential item to keep in your tackle box or the glove box of your car. The petroleum company Engen obligingly produces tide tables every year and they are available at your local Engen petrol station (usually early in the new year) for a nominal amount. Alternatively, tide tables are sometimes stocked by sports shops specializing in fishing tackle.

A typical galjoen spot at spring high (left) and low tide (right).

CHAPTER TWO

FISHING SKILLS

To be a successful angler, understanding when and why fish bite is only the first step. Tackle and angler techniques such as knot-tying and casting will in turn enable the skilled angler to rise above the rest, especially when predatory species such as yellowtail are feeding madly and the action may be hectic but relatively shortlived. Under these circumstances the angler who has spent time checking and preparing his tackle and tying good knots, who knows where to position his lure or bait and how hard he can pull on his line, will consistently have better catches than the angler who pays attention to his tackle for the first time when he is at or on the sea.

UNDERSTANDING FISH BEHAVIOUR

When fishing from the beach you need the correct tackle, knowledge of beach formation and sea conditions, as well as adequate protective clothing.

To become a successful fisherman it is imperative that you come to grips with the behaviour of fish. In other words, *think like a fish*. Those anglers who do not bother with this aspect of fishing may strip to the waist and cast their lines in calm and clear water on a lovely sunny day but, apart from enjoying the sunshine and catching the odd *klipvissie* or shark, may land nothing worthwhile.

Fishing is not a hit or miss affair. If you want to catch fish you have to take the trouble to find out which fish are known to frequent what waters, the type of bait they respond to, when they feed and where specifically they go to find their food.

Fish – especially those that occur close to the shore in the intertidal zone – are more active when the water is churned up, as it provides cover for them to feed in the shallows, where most of the food is available. During calm and clear conditions fish seek shelter and come out to feed only when direct sunlight either has not yet reached, or has already left, the water – hence it is the early riser who is likely to return home with a catch. The fact that fish prefer murky water is the reason why even in rivers and estuaries the experienced angler will arrange his fishing trip to coincide with the rising tide. For example, mullet (harders) normally congregate near or in the mouths of rivers and will move into the shallows in the murky water ahead of the pushing tide.

In estuaries, shoals of spotted grunter move on to the prawn banks to feed as the tide rises.

Fishing for kob *(kabeljou)* is best on the rising tide until approximately one hour after high tide, and always in the discoloured water ahead of the clear water that is pushing in from the sea.

Estuarine species such as white steenbras (pignose grunter), spotted grunter and garrick (leervis) feed on or over prawn banks and on the edges of deep-water channels. Again, the incoming or high tide is most likely to produce the best results.

Species such as shad (elf) normally forage at first and last light, especially when conditions are calm and clear. However, when the sea is churned up and the water is milky they are likely to feed on the high tide during all hours of the day.

Surface feeders like tuna, yellowtail and 'couta (king mackerel) generally feed early in the morning or late in the afternoon. Boat anglers are often frustrated by the sight of shoals of predatory fish lazing about on the surface between mid-morning and mid-afternoon, refusing to take a bait or line that had caught fish very successfully a few hours earlier. Seabirds such as Cape gannets (*malgas*), terns (*sterretjies*) and whitechinned petrels feed on the baitfish that gamefish drive to the surface, and they are often seen rafting on the water in an area where gamefish were seen feeding earlier. The birds seem to know that the gamefish are still around, and it is well worth returning to the area later in the afternoon when the gamefish once again rise to the surface to feed.

READING THE CONDITIONS

Fishing conditions vary from day to day and no matter how much you may have spent on getting the best tackle or how fresh your bait may be, to make consistently good catches you must be able to read the conditions and to adapt your strategy accordingly.

The experienced angler can, merely by looking at the water, select the likely spot where his target species may be feeding. The spot he selects may depend on the season of the year, how 'open' or rocky a gully may be, the depth and colour of the water, the state of the tide, and how rough or calm the water is.

Before deciding where to fish from a beach, try to find some vantage point from which you can first study the area for productive-looking spots. Fish are often found in channels and holes in the sand that have been scoured out by currents or rough water (or on the sandbanks sliding into the channels and holes), but these features can shift or close in a matter of days, so that a spot you fish one week may not be there the next. These channels and holes are normally visible as darker coloured water where the incoming waves roll through instead of breaking. Shoals of kob, white steenbras or shad, as well as sharks, may be found feeding in such spots.

Avoid shallow, featureless beaches. These are usually in the lee of a headland and protected from the large swells. Because of the relatively calm water, therefore, the reefs are unlikely to be subjected to the scouring action of waves, nor will there be the holes and channels associated with more exposed beaches.

Do take time to read books on fishing. They will broaden your knowledge and will also give you new ideas to improve your strategy. Also, speak to as many anglers as possible, especially when fishing outside your home area. Anglers are always willing to give advice, and they may even tell you where or how to fish in their area.

Some of the more important aspects of fishing conditions are discussed in chapter one.

PREPARING THE TACKLE

A successful angling trip starts at home. Fishing gear such as rods and reels should be carefully checked to see that they are in good working order. Line too should be checked. If you have been rock or surf angling, it is most important to inspect the first 10 to 15 metres of line for nicks and abrasions. Cut them off if there are signs of wear or if the line has lost its elasticity. If you have been deep-sea angling, check the first 50 metres of line – particularly if you have hooked a fish and it has dived under the boat, causing the line to chafe against the keel.

A strong fighting fish such as the yellowtail will test both your skill and your tackle. In this instance the time spent on tackle preparation has been well rewarded.

TACKLE MAINTENANCE

Regular maintenance of fishing tackle, and of rods and reels in particular, should be ongoing.

The rod After a day's fishing, wash your rod down, clean the dirt and grit out of the reel seat and dry it off with a chamois. A rod should also be inspected for damage to the blank as well as the guides. In particular, check for worn or cracked guides, especially at the rod tip. These have been the reason for many a lost fish, especially when fishing with light tackle; and trolling for gamefish can become even more expensive when a snapped line had an expensive lure, such as a Rapala, tied to the end of it. Store the rod in a horizontal position, preferably on a rod rack in your garage, out of harm's way.

The reel Fishing reels should be serviced at least once or twice a season. If you are confident of your own mechanical ability, you can service your own reels by simply following the instructions on the supplier's brochure or pamphlet, but it is advisable to enlist somebody's help the first time, as sometimes it is not as easy as it looks. Alternatively, take your reels to a local tackle shop, or approach one of the 'old pros' at the club for some assistance.

To ensure that a reel is always in good condition it should be rinsed with fresh water as soon as possible after use but make sure that you tighten the drag so that water cannot penetrate to the inner parts of the reel. Spray it gently to wash off all salt and sand. Do not spray with a strong jet of water, as this is likely to force salt or sand particles into the reel. Wipe the reel dry and, before storing it, spray it with a light oil or a moisture-repellent product such as Q20 or WD40, but try not to coat the line.

Lastly, loosen the drag before storing the reel as, by leaving it tight, you compress the drag washers. This will ultimately make the drag stick and you stand a very good chance of 'popping' (breaking) the line, especially when fishing with light line.

Nylon line If nylon line is wound on to a spool under strain – for instance, when you are fighting a big fish, or when your line is caught on a reef – make sure you unwind most of the line at the end of the day's fishing, or preferably sooner. (Ask someone to take the end of the line and run it off on a large field, leave it for a while and then rewind.) Nylon that has been stretched, then wound on wet and allowed to dry in the sun, exerts tremendous pressure on the spool and if left on the reel is quite capable of bursting the spool, especially the older, bakelite spools.

With proper care and attention, you can ensure that your line does not let you down when you can least afford it.

Tackle box It is most important to clean and oil your tackle box after a day's fishing, as well as everything you carry in it. A closed, damp tackle box causes everything inside it that is metal to rust very quickly.

Next, the correct balance of tackle must be selected. It serves no purpose to use surf or estuary tackle to catch larger gamefish such as tuna. This may seem obvious but I have often seen anglers climbing on board with a rod that may be perfectly suitable but with a reel which, for example, has a totally inadequate drag system, insufficient line capacity, or a spool that will not stand up to the rigours of gamefishing.

If you are going deep-sea angling, it is vital that you check the drag setting of your reel, making sure that it is working perfectly smoothly, especially if you intend fishing with light line.

The amount of tackle and accessories you take with you will change with experience; beginners tend to take everything but the kitchen sink. With time and experience you will reduce the quantity until you are carrying only the essentials for a particular species or location.

FISHING KNOTS

The importance of selecting the correct knots and tying them properly cannot be over-emphasized. It is surprising how often one hears anglers discussing how a record fish was lost because the line broke. 'Line failure', as guilty anglers like to call it, may indeed be due to the line breaking but may equally be due to selecting the wrong knot for the job or tying the knot incorrectly. A knot is the weakest point of the line but by tying the correct knot properly and tightly you will certainly improve your chances of landing a real trophy fish. Keeping the line moist when pulling a knot tight (a little saliva is an excellent lubricant) makes a significant difference to the efficacy of a knot. It is a devastating feeling to lose a big fish but the frustration is doubled if, on pulling in your line, you find a little pigtail at the end of the hook trace, indicating that a knot has pulled loose.

SKILFUL CASTING

No matter what facet of angling you may choose to participate in, the ability to cast far and accurately is a very important skill to develop. With practice you should ultimately be able to place your bait or lure within a metre or two of where you intend it to land.

The art of casting an artificial lure such as a fly or a spinner from a moving boat at a shoal of fish feeding on the surface can be compared to the skill and accuracy required to shoot a running buck. The ability to allow for the forward movement of the boat as well as the shoal can come only with experience. Use every opportunity to practise this skill. (An empty sports field is ideal, though it will not prepare you for retaining your balance in a boat!) At the end of the day your ability to place your bait or lure in exactly the right place will mean the difference between a fair and an excellent catch.

Redbait is an excellent bait especially for such species as galjoen, blacktail, zebra and white musselcracker.

BAIT-COLLECTING

It is important to use good-quality bait and to present it correctly. The golden rule is the fresher the bait the better; the only exception to this is the use of 'matured' redbait (two or three days old) when fishing for galjoen. Some anglers swear by it. But even this exception is not a hard and fast rule, as on some days, for some inexplicable reason, the galjoen will bite more readily on freshly cut bait.

If collecting your favourite bait requires travelling long distances, or if it can be done only at a spring low tide, involve the family as it is fun for the kids and also can save you a lot of time!

When fishing from the rocks or a beach it is well worthwhile to walk around at low tide to see which types of bait grow on the rocks or can be found in the sand. Be sure not to exceed the bag limit for the species you are collecting and do not collect more than you expect to use.

Fishing from the shore or a boat with live bait such as mullet (harder) can be both rewarding and exciting. In calm conditions, or when small fish are ripping your cut bait apart before the bigger fish can get to it, swimming a live bait can produce excellent results. In this case, to catch live bait it is necessary to become adept at using a throw net. (See pages 92-3 for detailed instructions.)

PLANNING AND PREPARING

The most sensible manner in which to prepare for a trip is to gather as much information as possible about the locality you wish to visit and the types of fish you are likely to catch, depending on the time of year. Exactly where should you fish? Which is the best tide to fish on? What bait types are required and is there any special way in which they should be rigged? These are all questions that should be answered before you go.

Some anglers keep a logbook in which they record when and where they have been fishing, the catch made, the state of the sea, the water temperature, the tide, details of bait used and weather conditions, and so on. Recording such information over several years not only makes interesting reading but also helps in planning future trips.

Careful planning and preparation do not only involve choosing a site and getting the tackle ready. Boat fishermen also need to check out the roadworthiness of their tow vehicle and trailer, especially if they plan to fish some distance from home.

An important factor that can affect your trip is the weather. A wind blowing from the wrong direction may make the sea cold, calm and clear and unfavourable for nearshore boat-fishing, and especially shore-fishing. If you are planning to fish far away from home, be sure to check weather conditions at your destination before setting out.

There is no fun in spending a weekend cooped up inside with gale force winds and stormy seas outside.

In the case of boat fishing, preparation must be taken a step further. Before each trip the boat and, if it is to be transported on a trailer, the tow vehicle should be carefully checked. The tyres of tow vehicles and trailers are prone to deflate when left standing. Check the battery of the tow vehicle as well as those of the boat. Switch on the radios and all the electronic navigation and fish-finding equipment and check that they are in good working order. Make sure that the life jackets, capsize container and first-aid kit are on board and, more important, that your crew knows where they are stowed. Start and check the engines and controls. The consequences of neglecting to check any of the above equipment can be both expensive and disastrous.

BAIT OR LURE PRESENTATION

Ensuring that the lure or bait you select is presented in a manner that the fish will find most natural and attractive is the culmination of all the effort that went into planning and preparing for the trip.

The appearance of the bait is important. Bait must be made up to look as natural as possible, while the size of the bait as well as the hook should suit the size of the fish you aim to catch. Trolled baits must swim naturally. If you intend using a lure, look at the size and shape of the bait-fish that a gamefish may spew up and select a lure that closely resembles it.

Lure selection is also important. Some lures are more successful on a dull, overcast day and others work better on a bright, sunny day. Usually a dull-coloured lure (black or blue) is used on a dull day, while brightly coloured lures are more effective on clear, sunny days. Don't be afraid to experiment, though, for while there are guidelines that may be followed for lure selection there are no hard and fast rules.

Keep in mind that the way in which you store a lure may affect its swimming action. A made-up lure should be stored in a tray by itself and not in a pile of other made-up lures. Putting each lure in its own plastic bag also works. The depth at which Rapala-type lures swim may be adjusted by bending the metal flap up or down. Have an expert show you how to adjust them to swim properly.

There are many patterns in which lures can be trolled behind a boat. They are dealt with in great detail in many of the overseas fishing magazines. Read all the articles you can lay your hands on and experiment with the patterns that may suit your type of fishing. Remember that the wake of the boat, the type of lure and the trolling speed will have an effect on exactly where you should position your lures. (See chapter 8 for specific information on lure-fishing.)

A good fishing strategy is to 'steal' with your eyes. If you are fishing next to an angler who is pulling out fish after fish while you are catching nothing there is a good chance that he may be using bait that differs from yours, that his tackle may be lighter, that his hook and sinker traces may be rigged differently or that he is casting his bait in a spe-cific spot. Fishing next to such an angler from a boat may be even more frustrating: he may, for example, be using a particular coloured lure that you do not have in your tackle box. Learn to watch closely. Try to copy his rig or, if you do not have the same colour or type of lure, use something similar and make a mental note to get one as soon as you can. Train yourself to continuously look and learn.

A selection of Rapala lipped lures.

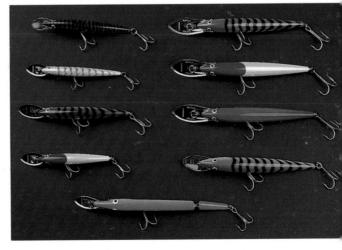

CHAPTER THREE

TACKLE

RODS

1. 'Banana butt', roller guide gamefishing rod and reel. 2. & 3. Stand-up gamefishing rods and reels. 4. & 5. Spinning rods and reels for boat fishing. 6. Scarborough spoonfishing rig. 7. Saltwater fly-fishing rod and reel. 8. Bait-casting rod and reel. 9. Open-face spinning rod and reel. 10. Closed-face spinning rod and reel.

Some years ago the average False Bay angler owned a 3,2- to 3,5-metre fibreglass (glass fibre) rod and a trusty Penn 49 reel (one of the early American slow-retrieval, multiplying gear reels). This set of tackle was used for all types of shore fishing, including spinning for yellowtail from ledges. When boat fishing, especially ski-boat fishing, became popular the shore spinnermen took this very same set of tackle to sea to spin for yellowtail and tuna. Although yellowfin tuna of 50 kilograms and over were landed on this reel with its bakelite spool and 160 metres of 18-kilogram breaking-strain line, many a story was told of spools 'popping' while the angler was fighting these big fish.

Nowadays a staggering, and often confusing, selection of equipment and brand names faces the prospective buyer.

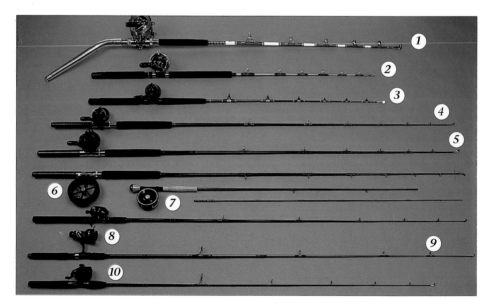

FIBREGLASS VS. GRAPHITE

Fibreglass rods today face stiff competition from graphite (carbon-fibre) rods, which offer several advantages over fibreglass, depending on the grade of graphite used in the manufacturing process. Naturally, the better the quality of graphite the greater the advantages – and the more expensive the rod.

Graphite rods are not only 25 to 33 percent thinner walled and therefore lighter than fibreglass, but they are also four times stronger. When flexed (as when fighting a fish), a graphite rod will return to its original shape much more quickly than a fibreglass rod, enabling the angler to wind in a vital few more centimetres of line when 'pumping' his fish – particularly a gamefish. Similarly, the loading up, or bending, of a graphite rod when making a long cast, and its quick return to its straight shape accelerate the propulsion of the sinker, enabling the angler to cast further. The light construction of a graphite rod, irrespective of its length, makes it more sensitive to a fish's movements and, of course, it is less tiring to fish with. That said, a graphite rod is more brittle and less resistant to bumps and knocks than a fibreglass rod. It is also a potentially lethal conductor of electricity and should not be fished with during an electric storm!

Rods are also manufactured from a combination of fibreglass and graphite. Fibreglass gives the rod strength while the graphite content makes it lighter and more sensitive. For some it can be the happy medium in terms of price and durability.

Select the rod and reel best suited to the type of fishing you intend to do. Here an angler fights a yellowtail from the ledges at Rooikrans, Cape Point.

REELS

Improvements in engineering and materials have also resulted in stronger, more reliable reels in recent years, but the three most popular types of reels have changed little in basic design and function.

THE MULTIPLYING REEL

As its name suggests, this design of reel is geared to multiply the number of times the spool rotates for each turn of the handle. Reels are available with ratios ranging from 3:1 to as high as 6:1. The higher ratios are a definite advantage when you are fishing among reefs and you need to lift your hook and sinker as quickly as possible to prevent them from getting stuck.

Fitted on top of the rod, this type of reel has a revolving spool and a clutch which is disengaged when casting. To prevent the spool from overwinding, resulting in a tangled mess of line when casting, it is necessary to impart gentle pressure to the spool with the thumb – a technique that is only perfected with practice.

For open-sea fishing, multiplying reels offer several advantages over other types, such as strength of spool, the capacity to hold a lot of line and a large drag surface to give a good drag system – all essential features when fighting a large fish.

THE OPEN-FACE FIXED-SPOOL REEL (COFFEE GRINDER)

This is the reel normally used to introduce young anglers or newcomers to fishing as it is difficult to achieve an overwind with this reel. Once the timing of when to let the line go when casting has been mastered, it is easy to use. However, it is not a reel just for novices. It is frequently preferred by experienced anglers when fishing in estuaries, as it makes casting a light bait or lure much easier and the presentation of the bait is far more natural and appealing to the fish.

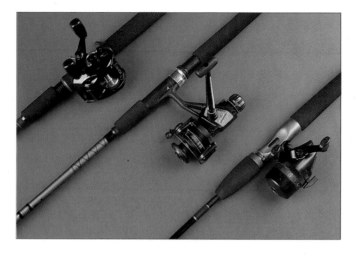

From the left: A light tackle bait casting reel, an open-face spinning reel and a closed-face spinning reel.

Fitted below the rod, with the spool mounted sideways, the line on this reel is wound on to a fixed spool by means of a metal bale arm which revolves as the handle turns to feed the line on to the spool, rather like winding it on by hand. To cast, the bale arm is moved aside, which allows the line to run off the spool with hardly any friction. This is why very light lines and bait can be cast some distance with this type of reel, and for this reason it is often the choice of the experienced angler when fishing in estuaries. Remember, though, that the line will loop or twist as it unwinds from the spool, so it is necessary to use a rod with larger than normal guides close to the spool in order to facilitate the smooth, unhampered flow of the line.

THE CLOSED-FACE FIXED-SPOOL REEL

This reel works on the same principle as the open-face reel, is just as simple to use but does not have a bale arm. The line is released simply by depressing a button on the back of the reel. To retrieve the line, any movement of the handle engages the retrieval mechanism. It usually has a star drag system that works on the same principle as that of multiplying reels.

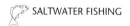
THE CENTRE-PIN (SCARBOROUGH) REEL

The universally popular multiplying reel (left) and (right) the Scarborough, which is still one of the most popular reels used by the shore as well as the boat anglers of Natal.

In its simplest form this type of reel has no clutch, drag system or gears and consists of a narrow spool which normally has two handles and turns on a metal spindle. The reel is fished below the rod and the retrieval speed depends on the size of the spool and how fast you turn the handle!

Although of a simple construction, it is not so simple to use, yet it is still one of the most popular reels used by the shore as well as the boat anglers of KwaZulu-Natal. Skilled users maintain that they are more 'in touch' with the fish and therefore are more confident when hooking and fighting a fish. There is certainly an art to casting with a Scarborough, particularly on a crowded groyne or jetty during a shad (elf) run.

When fishing for bottom fish in deep water, boat anglers from the eastern Cape and KwaZulu-Natal prefer to use the large diameter Scarboroughs: they are robust, and quick and easy to use as no casting is involved. Many Cape sport anglers, on the other hand – old diehards, in particular – prefer handlines, but these are apt to tangle, especially when the line has lost its elasticity. These anglers nonetheless claim that by using a handline they are even more in touch with the fish, but then they do not have to contend with the strong currents of the eastern Cape and KwaZulu-Natal waters.

When fishing in deep water with a rod and a Scarborough reel the hook is set by winding the fish on, as the stretch in the length of line makes it difficult to set it by striking.

It goes without saying that very few anglers are now prepared to use the earlier range of multiplying reels with their brittle bakelite spools, slow retrieval rates and inefficient drag systems. Today's angler wants a reel that is sturdy, reliable, capable of holding a good amount of line, having a high gear ratio for quick retrieval and with a smooth-as-silk drag. Reels that meet all these criteria are generally expensive but they do enable the angler to do battle with, and land, far larger fish on lighter line classes with 2-, 4- and 6-kilogram breaking strain.

As with all fishing tackle, there are many combinations of rods and reels that are not as expensive as the top-of-the-range models and which will adequately serve their purpose. Nevertheless, it is advisable to avoid the cheap end of the market. There are many low-priced imitations of the expensive varieties but you will discover that they are made of inferior materials. Cheap rods have thin walls and poor quality guides that wear quickly. Cheap reels will not take the strain of normal use – the body of the reel may crack when bumped on a rock, and the mechanical parts usually wear quickly and cannot be replaced, as no spares are available. It is therefore important to assess the features and quality of each item and buy the best you can afford. To lose a really big fish when a reel seizes or a rod breaks for no apparent reason is an experience to avoid.

Seek advice from a knowledgeable angler and buy well-known brands, as spares and servicing facilities for these are generally available at reputable tackle dealers.

To discuss the pros and cons of each type of rod and reel available on the market is a near-impossible task, but the following summary will give an indication of the more popular combinations used for rock and surf, estuarine and gamefish angling.

ROCK AND SURF ANGLING

The casual rock and surf angler has the choice of having either one rod and reel that will generally serve the purpose, or two sets that should enable him to compete on a more equal footing with the more experienced angler. How often you wish to fish in the company of regular surf anglers without being frustrated by the fact that you cannot reach the distance they are casting will therefore influence how many sets of rods and reels you have.

Should the choice be to purchase only one rod and reel, a rod approximately 3,5 metres in length with a 115-gram (4-ounce) tip should suffice. This length of rod is suitable to use off rocks and ledges as well as for surf fishing. The more experienced angler prefers to use surf rods 4,1 to 4,5 metres in length with a 170-gram (6-ounce) tip, which allows longer-distance casting of a heavy sinker and bait; to be able to cast a long distance is a definite advantage especially when fishing on a gently shelving beach. In contrast with surf fishermen, rock or gully fishermen prefer to use a shorter rod of about 3,5 metres in length. This length of rod allows short but accurate casts among the rocks.

Many reels match the above-mentioned rods but one multiplying reel with a line capacity of approximately 300 metres of 12- or 14-kilogram breaking-strain line could be used for both fishing from the rocks and in the surf.

ESTUARINE ANGLING

The keen estuary or lagoon angler will insist that at least one set of spinning tackle and one set of baitfishing tackle is the minimum required for the job.

Spinning rods normally vary in length between 1,8 and 2,4 metres and are of single- or two-piece design. The rod tip is light, to enable the casting of small spinners or lures, but stiffens quite rapidly into the butt. The guides on the rod are larger than normal, especially the one closest to the reel, to accommodate a spinning reel or 'coffee grinder', as they are commonly called. The spinning reels are very simple to operate and are most suitable for light-line classes up to 6 kilograms. They have fast retrieval speeds and a good drag system and can cast a light or heavy lure with ease.

Bait-casting rods are normally heavier than spinning rods and are used with a revolving drum reel which is often fitted with a level-wind mechanism. Most of these reels have a magnetic cast control and an outstanding drag system. The rods are 1,5 to 1,8 metres long, slightly heavier in the tip and have a slower taper than the spinning rods. As a result there is less whip in the rod when casting and less chance of an overwind. These rods and reels are also very popular with inshore boat anglers as they can handle large fish such as kob and that excellent fighter, the yellowtail.

Estuarine angling – the most tranquil and relaxing form of salt-water fishing.

33

DEEP–SEA ANGLING

In comparison with all the other methods of angling, gamefish (and particularly deep-sea) angling has the largest variety as well as the most expensive tackle on offer. Here a line needs to be drawn between the requirements of a casual angler and a dedicated tournament fisherman. While the casual angler may have one or maybe two sets of trolling gear as well as a spinning rod, the tournament angler inevitably ends up with as many as two or even three sets of tackle for each of the IGFA (International Gamefishing Association) line-class categories in which he chooses to compete.

Apart from the specialized 'banana butt' or bent butt rods specifically designed to use in a fighting chair, there are two types of deep-sea trolling rods. The earlier trolling rods were longer and stiffer and had a much slower taper than the more popular, shorter (2- to 2,5-metre) stand-up rods which have now cornered the market. Although the older style of rod could be used when standing up or in a fighting chair, it was awkward and heavy, and when used with the earlier types of shoulder harness, quite capable of reducing the strongest person to tears when fighting a big fish from a standing position. The stiff rod and the shoulder harness tended to pull the shoulders forwards, causing the muscles in the small of the back as well as the hamstrings to seize up.

The stand-up rig has now swung the balance of power in favour of the angler. When the appropriate harness and bucket combination is used with a short 'stand-up' rod matched with a quick-retrieving lever drag reel, experienced gamefishermen are capable of taking on the really large billfishes such as marlin and broadbill swordfish.

For some anglers the most exciting form of gamefishing is casting a spinner or any other surface lure at gamefish feeding on the surface. To see a gamefish such as a

Gamefishing at its best: a sailfish being held by the bill prior to being tagged and released.

yellowfin tuna clear the water in an attempt to swallow the spinner is a thrilling sight, but best of all is the take. The angler can feel the strike and the strength of the fish as it peels off line, in contrast to watching the action in a detached way when the rod is resting in a rod holder.

There are two easily defined schools of spinning anglers and both can be defined in terms of region as well as tackle selection. First, there are the tuna and yellowtail anglers of the Cape, where short rods and multiplying reels are the rule. Rods are usually 2,4 to 2,8 metres long, while multiplying reels with a retrieval rate of 4,5:1 or higher, a spool capable of withstanding pressure and, most important, a smooth drag system are recommended. How heavy or light the combination of rod and reel is depends on the class of line the angler wishes to use and the size of fish he hopes to land.

The banana butt rod specifically designed to use in a fighting chair. The reel has an enormous line capacity and a smooth and efficient lever drag system.

In KwaZulu-Natal, there is quite a different breed of spinning anglers, who prefer the centre-pin Scarborough reel. They will assure you that once you have fought through the hangups of monstrous overwinds, burnt hands and limited casts, the reel begins to come into its own. Its 1:1 retrieval rate is made acceptable by its spool diameter, the ideal size for spinning being 18 centimetres. (This is not to be confused with the bottom-fishing version of the reel, which is far heavier and not conducive to casting at all.) Mated to a more flexible rod of about 2,5 metres long in order to impart a very erratic darting action to the spoon (which is said to be what makes the fish excited), the Scarborough is cast with one of three or four specialized methods, best learned by watching an experienced Scarborough angler at work.

Whether you follow the Cape or the KwaZulu-Natal tradition, the guidance of an experienced spinner fisherman will be an advantage when selecting correctly balanced tackle.

LINES

The technical advances that have taken place in the extrusion of nylon line leaves the angler with a wide choice of colour, suppleness, durability, line diameter and breaking as well as knot strengths. The selection of a type or brand depends on which of the above qualities the individual angler feels will best suit his form of fishing.

The choice of the casual angler will more than likely be the happy medium, which is a moderate line diameter, giving protection against wear and tear and having good knot-tying characteristics but not necessarily guaranteed to break at or below the stated breaking strain of the line. The tournament angler may elect to use a line of thinner diameter, which the manufacturer guarantees will break at or below the given breaking strain. This line normally has less stretch in it and has to be handled more carefully. Yet some tournament anglers maintain that they are more in touch with the fish when using this line and,

A selection of popular lines and traces.

provided the drag of the reel is set correctly and no fingers sneak on to the spool to stop the line, they feel they have a better chance of landing the fish.

For rock and surf fishing there is no need to change the line unless you are dissatisfied with it or it is showing obvious signs of wear and tear. The upper 50 metres or so will, with regular use, lose its colour and stretch, and may break while the angler is trying to free traces stuck in the rocks or when he is fighting a big fish. The broken piece of line can be cut back – provided there is sufficient line left on the spool – or the line wound off the reel and reversed, bringing the unused line to the top of the spool.

Your choice of line may also be influenced by the distance you wish to cast. If the best conditions for a species mean that you have to regularly cast into the wind, a line of thinner diameter may give that extra distance you need. With the thinner-diameter line your casting action must be very smooth as you stand a good chance of snapping the line, especially when attempting to cast a big bait. The margins for error when using light line are slim.

BUYING LINE

Fishing line may be the cheapest item that you purchase but it plays a very important role in successful angling, so don't stop short at buying good quality. Cheap line is false economy. It will either break well below the stated breaking strain, or above. In the latter case, competition anglers can have their catch or record disqualified if the line is found to have a greater breaking strain than stated. Another disadvantage of cheap line is that it is prone to snap anywhere along its length when you try to break free after getting stuck. Rather buy the best line you can afford and replace it at least once a season in the case of casual angling, and more regularly in the case of light-line or tournament fishing.

TRACES

Surf fishermen as a rule use thicker hook and sinker traces because of the pronounced body action and power that goes into the cast. It is most frustrating to break a sinker trace and to end up unplucking an overwind when everyone else is landing fish around you. Some anglers also prefer to use a thicker nylon hook trace instead of a short steel-wire trace when fishing for shad (elf).

When fishing from ledges or in rocky gullies it is best to use thinner hook and sinker traces. This type of fishing tends to lead to the loss of many a hook and sinker, and thin traces tend to break at the swivel, minimizing the loss of great lengths of main line.

The exception to the above would be when you are fishing for large bottom feeders in rocky gullies and you need to keep the fish away from rocks and crevices. Under these conditions it is best to use a very thin sinker trace and a strong hook trace: the sinker trace will break free very easily and the thicker hook trace gives the angler the upper hand when bringing a large fish to the gaff. Some 30 years ago most offshore anglers used low-stretch braided Dacron and single-strand (or piano wire) or multi-strand (7- or 49-strand) wire traces. Today's offshore anglers use predominantly IGFA-rated nylon with heavier nylon traces for species such as billfish and tuna.

The wahoo – a member of the 'razor gang', quite capable of destroying lures and biting off nylon or thin steel traces.

Wire traces are still used when fishing for the 'razor gang' species such as wahoo, 'couta (king mackerel) and sharks. The wire – an adaptation of piano wire and readily available in tackle shops – can be bought in different diameters, from numbers 2 to 15. For the aforementioned species, the correct size is between 4 and 9. The thinner wire is used on the leader in front of the bait, tied to a swivel; the thicker wire is then used to tie the hooks on, where the teeth are going to bite. (See page 147.)

NOTE *Traces made from multi-strand wire are crimped on with special metal crimps and a crimping tool but those made from single-strand piano wire are tied on with the haywire twist. Crimps, armour springs and eyelets are also available for nylon traces.*

LURES AND SPINNERS

There is one common weakness that most lure fishermen share and that is the compulsive buying of practically every new lure that appears on the market – and who can blame them? The striking colours of the lures along with posters of desperate fish leaping out of the water to grab them are enough to have most of us reaching for our wallets in the hope that *this* is the ultimate lure. The end result is a tackle box – and sometimes even a tackle cupboard – stacked with lures that may never have seen the light of day.

However, no matter how many lures and spinners gamefishermen may possess, they tend to have a few favourites which they will use each time they go fishing, and although they are quite happy to experiment with new or different lures, they usually revert to their old faithfuls should the new lures not produce positive results quickly enough.

Lures can be roughly divided into three categories: those that splash or perform on the surface, those that 'swim' with a good, lively action on the surface, and the subsurface lures that simulate or resemble the swimming action of baitfish.

Lures that splash or perform on the surface are the Kona variety. Typically, they have a flat or concave face which causes the lure to dive and return to the surface, or splash while it is being trolled at a relatively fast speed (about 8 knots) in an upright position. The bigger varieties of this lure are used for billfish such as marlin, while smaller-sized Konas are usually used on calm, windless

days, when gamefish such as yellowfin and longfin tuna are loath to strike at lures trolled on or below the surface.

There is an endless variety of lures available for the smaller gamefish such as tuna, skipjack, yellowtail and dorado. To be successful it is important to have a selection of both different colours and different sizes of lures. On certain days gamefish may be feeding on smaller or larger types of baitfish, and not being able to vary the size of the lure may culminate in a very frustrating and unsuccessful day's fishing.

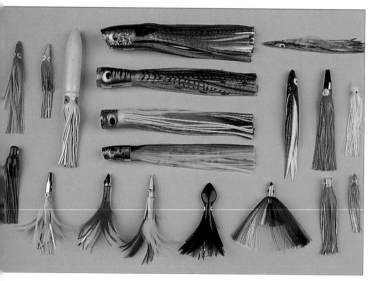

A selection of lures for gamefishing.

Colours are important. For example, the longfin tuna caught off the Cape Peninsula favour green and yellow, red and white, and red and blue lures. This does not mean that other colours will not work on a particular day, although few of the local anglers will go to sea without the above selection in their tackle boxes.

The range of colours, sizes and types of lures that you keep in your tackle box may depend largely on the popularity of certain types of lures among local anglers, but don't be afraid to experiment, as fish are unpredictable and have been known to strike on the most unlikely lure.

Subsurface lures such as the lipped Rapala are highly effective but are capable of creating the most horrific tangle of trolled lures if they are not swimming properly. Make sure that you are capable of 'tuning' them (that is, adjusting the angle of the lip to make the lure wobble and swim in a straight line) as this will save you hours of labour undoing tangles and making up new leaders and traces, as well as help keep your blood pressure down! Subsurface lures are available in different sizes as well as an assortment of colours and it is well worth while keeping a selection in your tackle box. Bear in mind, though, that the well-sharpened treble hooks of this lure can be dangerous when a fish is landed.

If the action is fast and furious an angler may be tempted to leave a hooked fish on the deck while either casting with another rod or assisting another angler to gaff a fish. A treble hook hanging loose from a fish which is jumping about on the deck can very easily end up in the leg or hand of an unsuspecting angler. The way around this is to subdue the fish as soon as possible before carrying on. Not only is this safer but the quality of the flesh of a fish that has been quickly despatched is far superior to the flesh of one that has been left to thrash about on the deck or in the fish box.

Spinners and, more recently, plugs are normally used to cast at gamefish by anglers fishing from the shore or from a boat but they can also be trolled. (While lures are usually trolled, the speed of spinners and plugs is determined by the retrieval rate imparted by the angler.) The thinner variety, such as the 'snake' spinner used by boat fishermen off Cape Point when trolling for yellowtail, are known to

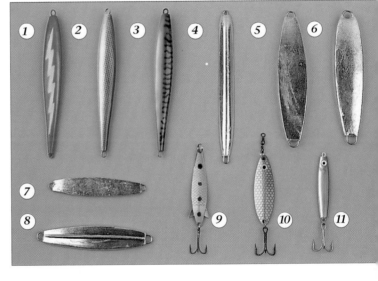

A range of spinners used by gamefishermen at sea and in estuaries.

1.& 2. Striker snoek.
3. Snake spinner.
4. Reid special.
5 & 6. Round back.
7 & 8. Mini Reid special.
9. Toby. 10. Abu-Koster.
11. Striker little monster.

be consistently successful. As in the case of lures, spinners are available in a variety of shapes and sizes and the selection you carry in your tackle box will depend on the proven success of certain types or designs and your ability to make them work by either bending them or varying the rod position and the retrieval rate to get the best swimming action.

Plugs are really wooden lures. They are flat or concave-shaped and are whipped or pulled along the surface to create plenty of action and white water. They are especially popular among the shore gamefishermen for species such as garrick and yellowtail.

SINKERS

The choice of sinker (commonly called a 'lead') used by an angler depends largely on the type or class of tackle being used, as well as the sea bed and the state of the sea.

The weight of the sinker you select will naturally depend on the class of tackle you are using, but fishing with the right shape of sinker is equally important. When you are fishing in a strong sea and over a rocky sea bed it is best to use a flat or rectangular sinker rather than the popular 'bottle'-shaped sinker which does not settle in one place but rolls around until it eventually gets stuck. In calm weather the fish may be keener to grab a bait which is moving about in the gully and in this case it may be more advantageous to use the bottle-type sinker.

When fishing off a beach or in sandy-bottomed gullies in lively or rough conditions, 'grab' or pyramid sinkers are ideal to anchor your gear. Although some species may strike more readily when the bait is moving about, it is difficult to fish, especially in a crowd or at night, when you are unsure of where exactly your bait has come to rest. (An angler using an ordinary sinker when everybody else is using a grab sinker and whose line tangles with everybody else's becomes very unpopular, to say the least!) Be sure to carry a variety of shapes and weights of sinkers appropriate to your tackle so that you will be able to fish from the shore in any condition.

Ball and barrel sinkers are used mainly by boat anglers to position a bait at a specific depth in the water column: for example, when fishing for Cape snoek, which are fond of biting off the bottom. This type of sinker is relatively small and unobtrusive and helps to present an attractive bait. To cast a small bait into calm water, gully fishermen also use ball sinkers which slide freely above the hook.

There are sinkers specifically made for boat anglers for fishing on the sea bed in varying conditions of depth and current. They come in a wide range of sizes, the largest weighing a kilogram. Remember, though, that although the heavier sinker allows the angler to reach the bottom with relative ease, the weight of the sinker makes it more difficult to feel the bite or take of the fish.

1. Spoon sinkers.
2. Bottle sinkers.
3. Cone sinker.
4. Pyramid sinker.
5. & 6. Grab sinkers.
7. Ball sinkers.
8. Barrel sinkers.
9. Boat sinkers.
10. A selection of swivels and clips.

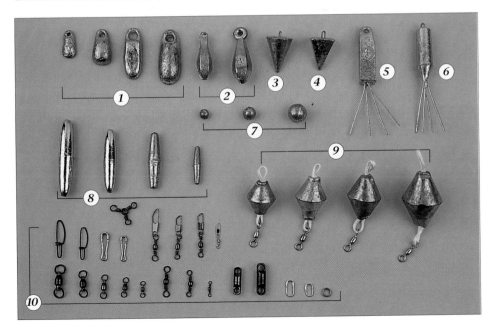

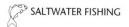
Heavy (1-kilogram) sinkers are commonly used along the eastern Cape coast and off KwaZulu-Natal where boat anglers have to contend with a strong current on most days. They are also used to take baits rigged for billfish, such as the broadbill swordfish, to the desired depth. These sinkers are 'sacrificed', as they drop away when a fish is hooked.

Sinkers may also form part of the lure, as in the case of the chromed lead or painted snoek dolly used by Cape snoek fishermen.

MAKING YOUR OWN SINKERS

Casting or moulding your own sinkers is very easy to do and can save you a lot of money. In addition to the lead and sinker moulds (moulds are usually available at tackle shops), you will need a pot in which to melt the lead, a metal ladle and a small stove. A good pair of gloves (welding gloves are ideal) are also necessary, as both the mould and the melting pot become very hot.

You will be surprised at the number of sinkers you can make in one afternoon.

SWIVELS AND CLIPS

The use of good-quality swivels and clips is as important as choosing the correct knots and tying them properly. Clips or connectors, such as stainless-steel split rings and oval clips, are available in a wide range of sizes and are used to attach treble hooks to spinners or Rapala-type lures. Take particular care of how you remove the trebles from the mouth of a fish, as twisting the lure or using brute force to free it can bend or even open the ring or clip and make it likely that you will lose a fish on the next strike. A good tip is to tie the knot of a nylon trace over the 'split' of the oval clip. This will prevent the clip from opening up when the angler is fighting a fish.

Two of the more common swivels used by deep-sea fishermen and shore anglers are the ball-bearing snap swivels (used for gamefish) and the barrel swivels (used by shore and boat anglers).

The ball-bearing snap swivels are used to troll baits and lures and are available in different sizes. The size of the swivel should match the tackle as well as the size of the lure or bait so as not to affect the action. Black swivels are preferred when fishing in tropical conditions where members of the 'razor gang' snatch at anything shiny. Many a lure, rigged on a wire trace, has been lost when a toothy species such as a wahoo has grabbed the shiny swivel and bitten through the nylon line above the swivel.

Barrel swivels are used to attach hook and sinker traces, as stoppers for running traces and as an attachment point for small lures and spinners when they are rigged with a trace for casting. Although barrel swivels do not rotate as well as the ball-bearing type, they do help to prevent the line from twisting, especially when trolling a spinner.

Barrel swivels fitted with a snap link are more suited to freshwater fishing and should not be used in the sea, especially when deep-sea fishing, as they are bound to open up on the strike, even if it is only a small gamefish such as a skipjack (bonito).

HOOKS

Fish hooks are available in a variety of shapes and sizes. They are made from different materials, such as bronzed or chromed mild steel and stainless steel, and in different thicknesses, which in turn determine the strength of the hook. The choice of hook is normally governed by the size of the fish you wish to catch, the size of its mouth and the size and type of bait you intend to use.

1. A range of tinned treble hooks. 2. Hooks for rock and surf fishing. 3. Southern tuna hook; sea demon; Kendal round (2 sizes). 4. (a-d) Mustad (different sizes); (e) silver barbless. (f) blued barbless.

Some manufacturers give the angler the choice of long- or short-shank hooks. The latter can be an advantage when fishing from the shore, as the smaller sizes, such as 1/0 and 2/0, are less prone to snapping during the fighting or landing of a large fish. The long-shank variety of the 1/0 and 2/0 hooks have been known to snap on the barb of the shank. The larger long-shank hooks, such as the 6/0, are very popular among anglers fishing for shad (elf). The longer shank helps to prevent bite-offs, especially when fishing with a nylon trace.

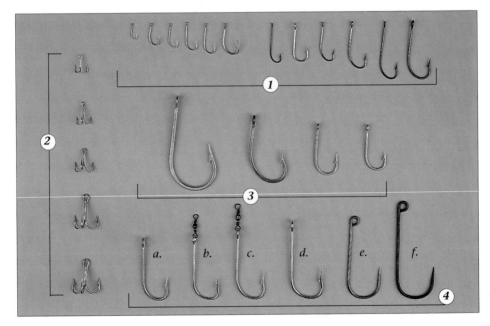

Treble hooks fitted by the manufacturers to spinners and swimming lures such as the Rapala are normally quite soft and bend open easily. Setting the drag too tight may result in losing a fish on the strike. When fishing for tuna it is best to use strengthened treble hooks and to make sure that they are sharp. When fishing with light tackle, hooks must be as sharp as possible because the drag setting of the reel is often not enough to set the hook. Check the sharpness of the hook with the thumbnail test: drag the hook across the thumbnail and if it is sharp enough it will stick or dig in; a blunt hook will just slide across the nail.

NOTE *Keep a small file or sharpening stone in your tackle box and regularly check the sharpness of all your hooks (including new ones). A well-honed point will improve your hook-up rate.*

TACKLE CONTAINERS

If you stroll among anglers at a popular fishing spot, you will be amazed by the types, shapes and sizes of the bags and boxes in which they carry their tackle. Shore anglers inevitably start off by carrying too much tackle but when they have to walk a long distance, especially in soft sand, they quickly regret their enthusiasm.

The first step in selecting the appropriate container is to determine whether it can hold all your essentials and still be comfortable to carry around. Rock and surf anglers normally like to use a soft bag or rucksack as lugging a tackle box over rough terrain or long distances is both uncomfortable and impractical.

A novel way of carrying tackle, especially when fishing off the rocks and walking long distances, is to wear a belt to which three or four plastic jars have been attached. All 'consumables' such as hooks, sinkers, trace line and swivels are carried in one jar while the remaining jars are filled with different types of bait.

Carrying the rest of your tackle – as well as food and water – in a rucksack means that everything can be kept out of harm's way while you are fishing on ledges or in gullies where the tide or waves can easily wet your bag or even wash it away.

A tackle box is not practical when fishing from rocks or off the beach: the box is frequently left open and a wave

Live-bait container (far left) and a selection of tackle and lure boxes.

splashing into it – or merely the exposure of the contents to the salty sea air – will cause the hooks and accessories in the box to rust. Even worse, if the wind is blowing, the tackle in the individual compartments may become covered in moist sea sand. The old army-type rucksack containing a few small, clear-plastic containers in which you store your hooks and swivels is, to my mind, the simplest and most practical way to fish off the rocks or beach.

Tackle boxes are, however, ideally suited to the needs of estuary and boat anglers who in general carry a far wider selection of tackle than that required by the rock and surf angler. These boxes are available in a variety of shapes, sizes and prices and can have one or a number of drawers. Each drawer has several compartments which may differ in size and in which lures, spinners, hooks, swivels, clips and trace line are kept, along with other essentials such as a knife, a pair of pliers, a hook sharpener, a pair of polarized sunglasses, a small screwdriver, a spanner for the reels, a tube of oil and – most important – a sunscreen and lip balm for protection against the sun.

The list of what to carry in your box is, in fact, endless and is limited only by the size of the box. It goes without saying that the tackle box you select should be made of sturdy, corrosion-proof material and should close securely.

Remember to pack all the heavier lures and accessories in the bottom of the box as a top-heavy tackle box, especially when left open, can fall over in the calmest of seas. The tackle box should never be left open on a seat or bunk if the angler is not nearby, as it is bound to end up on the deck, upside down.

Smaller boxes – small enough to slip into a bag or ruck-sack – with a few compartments to carry the lures and plugs used for estuarine angling are convenient to use, especially when the angler is wading in the shallows and a quick change of lure is required.

There are several roll-up-type lure bags on the market containing plastic-windowed pouches for the storage of lures. The individual pouches prevent the lures from tangling and allow for quick and easy selection.

ROD BUCKETS AND HARNESSES

Rod buckets.

Padded covers and bags for rods and reels are available at most tackle shops. These prevent the rods and reels from being damaged or scratched in the car or on the back of a truck when being transported to the boat or fishing spot, as well as on the boat when running to the fishing grounds. They are definitely a worthwhile invest-ment considering the cost of replacing tackle, especially those top-of-the-range, gold-coloured reels!

A soft leather rod bucket is ideal to use when fishing from rocks or the beach, especially when you need to hold a rod for long periods. Apart from taking the strain off the arms, a rod bucket also stabilizes the butt end of the rod, which makes fighting and landing a big fish that much easier.

A gimbal rod bucket is an essential part of the armoury of a boat angler. The gimbal fitting, normally made out of stainless steel, is a short tube with a cross pin at the back into which the recessed cross of the rod butt fits snugly. The gimbal itself swivels in a vertical direction, while the cross pin keeps the rod and reel upright, allowing the

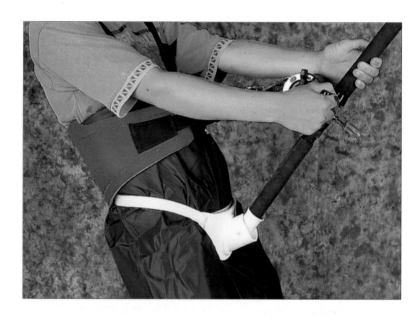

The stand-up harness. (Note that the rod bucket normally used with this harness has a wider base to spread the load or pressure over the angler's thighs.)

angler to use his arms to control the fish rather than having to hold and support the tackle.

Gamefishing rod buckets are wider and sturdier than leather rod buckets and are designed to spread the load across the thighs rather than centring it on the groin area. Anyone who has fought a large gamefish without this type of rod bucket can truly say that he learnt the hard way!

The rod bucket of a 'stand-up' rig differs from other rod buckets in that it is attached to a harness and hangs lower than the standard rod bucket, thereby lowering the pivot point and allowing the angler to hold a short rod higher up on the grip. The 'stand-up' technique enables the angler to put more and constant pressure on the fish with very little strain on the angler's back. This purpose-built rod bucket and harness, used by experienced gamefish anglers, helps to make it possible to do battle with large tuna and billfish while the angler is standing up, a feat many anglers would have considered impossible not so long ago.

PROTECTIVE CLOTHING

No matter what form of fishing you choose to participate in, protective clothing in one form or another is a must. The South African climate is such that the angler spends most of his time at the sea in bright, hot, sunny conditions, and it is therefore important to protect the skin against the harmful rays of the sun.

Most anglers wear some form of head gear – often quite unique in appearance. Wide-brimmed or floppy sun hats, although not as popular as peaked caps, provide the best protection, especially to the ears, neck and the back of the head. Gamefishermen, who spend the best part of their day peering into the water or scanning the horizon for the telltale white specks of birds hovering above a shoal of feeding fish, prefer peaked caps, as the peak helps to eliminate the glare reflected by the sea's surface. A good pair of polarizing sunglasses is essential for all types of fishing as it not only improves the angler's vision but helps to relieve eye strain.

Your choice of protective clothing should suit the local climate. Protective gear such as waders and a warm waterproof jacket will be distinctly uncomfortable to wear when fishing along the coast of KwaZulu-Natal, while a long-sleeved shirt and a pair of tracksuit pants to put on should it get cold will certainly not keep you dry! There is nothing more uncomfortable, especially when fishing off the beach, than to be wet and to have sand in your shoes and your clothes. A pair of lightweight, weatherproof pants will help to keep the sand out, especially if you have to kneel down when you tackle up or put on fresh bait.

Irrespective of the climate in which you are fishing, a sudden shower of rain is liable to chill you. A lightweight spray jacket that folds into a small bundle and is easy to store and carry should complete your outfit. Fine nylon, weatherproof pants-and-jacket outfits are also

Moulded boot waders.

51

ideal to use for boat fishing in warmer climates, as the combination of wind and spray or a sudden rain squall can leave you cold and miserable. For colder climates, a lightweight spray jacket or oilskin top should keep the angler warm and dry all day.

When fishing from the beach in warm weather, it is always a temptation to go barefoot and to wear shorts, but when wading in to cast there is always the chance of being stung by a bluebottle, particularly if an onshore wind has been blowing, so some form of protection for the legs and feet is advisable. (Some people react so violently to the sting of these creatures – even suffering total paralysis – that it is not worth taking a chance.) To prevent chafing of the feet, wear a pair of socks with your beach shoes.

Moulded boot waders are popular with beach anglers in the southwestern Cape and are also worn by rock anglers, especially when fishing for galjoen in the heart of the Cape winter. But these waders are extremely dangerous to wear when fishing from a boat. Should you fall overboard you would have very little chance of surviving, as they would undoubtedly fill up with water before you were able to remove them. Shore anglers should also be careful when wading out from the beach to cast, as stepping into a hole or being swamped by a wave could be equally dangerous.

Protective clothing for deep-sea or big-game angling should be chosen with care, as what you wear can affect your ability to fight a fish. Your clothing should be loose fitting and comfortable and must suit the local conditions. It is sometimes necessary to fight a big fish for hours on end and being dressed up in a thick or badly ventilated jacket may create perspiration and chafing problems which the tiring angler can certainly do without. A well-ventilated but waterproof jacket, preferably with a zip, is ideal, as it is easy to put on or remove even while fighting a fish.

ADDITIONAL EQUIPMENT

Apart from the essential tackle required on a fishing trip, there are certain important additional items that can have a direct bearing on the success of your trip.

GAFFS

Gaffs are essential items of equipment for boat fishermen. No ski- or gamefishing boat should put to sea without at least three or four gaffs on board, ideally two short ones and two sturdy, long-handled ones. A double or, even better, a 'full-house' strike of gamefish could end up in chaos should everyone attempt to bring their fish to the boat at the same time. Having a selection of short- and long-handled gaffs on board allows each angler to gaff his own fish if nobody is available to assist. It normally requires two gaffs to lift on board a gamefish larger than, say, 40 kilograms.

When gaffing fish from a boat it is best to gaff a fish in the back, preferably behind the head, and not from below, as a gaff through the belly tends to tear out easily.

Never be over-hasty to gaff a fish. If it is very large the anxious angler may be tired and urge you, the gaffer, to take a chance. Don't! Waiting a bit longer and making sure that the fish is gaffed properly is more of a help to the angler than 'tickling' the fish and extending the fight by another hour. Once a fish has been 'tickled', or mis-gaffed, it becomes boat shy and is reluctant to come close to the boat again. Many a record fish has been lost by either the angler becoming impatient to land the fish and pulling too hard, or the gaffer becoming over-eager to correct his earlier miss and mis-gaffing again.

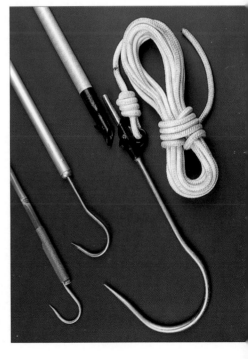

Typical boatgaffs with (right) a flying gaff.

Make sure that you are properly balanced and braced when you prepare to gaff a big fish from a boat. If you are off-balance the sudden lunge of a big fish is quite capable of pulling the gaff out of your hands or even pulling you overboard should you be foolish enough to hang on!

When fishing from ledges high above the sea, a long gaff is an essential accessory.

If you plan to fish for large gamefish, such as marlin or broadbill swordfish, a flying gaff is essential. The hook of a flying gaff has a rope attached to it, which in turn is attached to a sturdy point on the boat. The hook breaks free from the gaff pole when the fish is gaffed and the fish is brought to the side of the boat by the gaffer pulling on the rope.

If possible, leave the gaffing to someone with experience, as gaffing a large gamefish can be nerve-racking for a beginner: the presence of the fish, handling the trace and making sure that you gaff the fish in the correct spot certainly get the adrenalin pumping. Should there be no one else available, make sure that you wait until the fish is within reach of the gaff. When the opportunity arises, set the gaff in the back and as close to the head as possible. Most important of all, be sure you are not standing in the bight of the rope as you may be injured should the fish suddenly dash off once it has been gaffed.

Gaffs used by shore anglers vary in size. Beach fishermen usually keep handy a short (1,5-metre) gaff to land large kob or shark. It is often quite difficult to guide a fish on to the beach, especially when there is a ridge or lip on the edge of the beach. Under these conditions a short gaff is most suitable.

Anglers fishing from rocks, ledges or piers for species such as poenskop (black musselcracker) and yellowtail use a fairly long gaff (up to 3 metres) to land a fish when they are standing away from the water's edge. Rope gaffs are used by anglers fishing from harbour walls, cliffs or piers in order to gaff their catch from a position as high as 10 or 15 metres above the level of the sea. Obviously, these structures or natural protrusions enable anglers to get their bait out to where the big fish swim, but unless the fish can be walked to a more accessible area, the gaffing has to be executed under often extremely difficult conditions. Imagine trying to gaff a still-active 20-kilogram 'couta from a height of 10 metres!

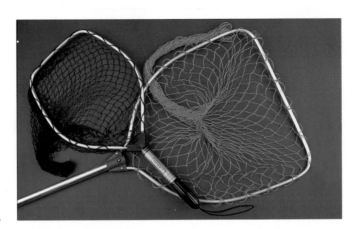

Landing nets.

LANDING NETS

Light-tackle anglers, especially those fishing in the relatively calm waters of an estuary or from a small boat, prefer to use a landing net instead of a gaff to secure their catch. As some of their target species are somewhat smaller but still difficult to boat or beach on a light line, landing them in a net is simpler and more efficient.

As with gaffing, it is important to wait for the correct moment, when the fish rises to the surface and is within reach. Try to avoid stretching for or snatching at the fish as either way you may scare the fish or even snap your line.

HEADLAMPS

Fishing at night without sufficient light in which to make up traces, put on bait and generally see what you are doing is definitely not a fun experience. A headlamp not only provides illumination but leaves both hands free.

A big torch or lamp standing next to your tackle box or bag is very handy but is not practical when you are standing at the water's edge, out of the light, and you need to check your tackle before casting, or you are trying to see a fish in the water when landing it.

Headlamps for fishing at night, and light sticks for illuminating bait in the water.

There are two types of headlamps available. The first has a separate battery container which hooks on to a belt around the waist or can be kept in a pocket of your protective clothing. It uses up to four torch batteries and provides a very bright light, the only drawback being that the cord between the battery container and the light tends to hang near the face and may be distracting. The second type of headlamp uses four penlight batteries and does not cast as strong a light but has the advantage of being a single unit and therefore less cumbersome to use. Both serve their purpose and will certainly make fishing at night that much easier and more enjoyable.

KNIVES AND TOOLS

A good knife, along with a sharpener, will be found in the tackle box or fishing bag of most anglers. It is used for cutting bait and nylon traces, for gutting and sometimes for scaling a fish. Some anglers prefer to carry two knives, one for general-purpose cutting and a second for filleting. Remember to use a bait board when you cut bait or fillet a fish, as this helps to preserve the cutting edge of the knife. There is nothing more frustrating than trying to cut a delicate piece of bait or filleting a fish with a blunt knife.

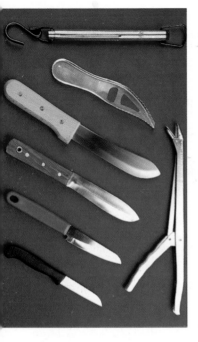

Above: A spring scale (top); a fish scaler and a selection of knives; a long-nosed hook extractor (right); ***Opposite:*** *The well- equipped surf angler.*

To scale fish, you can use the blunt or top edge of your knife but it is best to use a serrated metal scaler which is specially designed for the purpose. Nail clippers or a small pair of scissors are useful for cutting nylon traces and are handy to hang around the neck on a piece of string.

Many an angler can vouch for the pain caused by the spine of a barbel, and these anglers often carry a long-nosed hook extractor to remove the hook from the mouth of spiny or toothy species. If you do not wish to use a hook extractor, ask an experienced angler to demonstrate the correct method of handling the fish while retrieving the hook.

An extremely important and useful tool, pliers could solve the above problem, along with many others that are associated with boating. Jammed plugs, tight knots, loose nuts and a host of applications pertaining to safety can be attended to with a good pair, which can be carried in a special pouch on the belt. A pair of engineer's pliers are handy to remove the treble hooks of a spinner from the mouth of a gamefish, especially when you are in a hurry to get your spinner back into the water. Make sure that they are also strong enough to cut through the shank of a hook, if the point is stuck in someone's skin, so that the hook can be pulled out forwards without the barb catching.

ODDS AND ENDS

There are a number of small items which are not essential but complete the contents of the tackle box of the angler who likes to think he is prepared for any eventuality.

Experienced anglers include in their tackle box such items as a roll of dental floss (to bind over knots), a tube of lip balm and sunscreen (to protect the skin against the continuous glare of the sun), lotions to combat the sting of a blue bottle, and a small container of spare screws (for the reel or roller guides of gamefish rods).

CHAPTER FOUR

KNOTS AND RIGGING

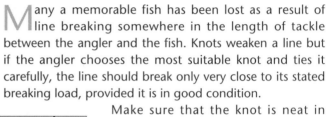

KNOTS

Fishing with a multiple-trace bottom rig is sure to test the angler's knot-tying ability.

Many a memorable fish has been lost as a result of line breaking somewhere in the length of tackle between the angler and the fish. Knots weaken a line but if the angler chooses the most suitable knot and ties it carefully, the line should break only very close to its stated breaking load, provided it is in good condition.

Make sure that the knot is neat in appearance; a neat knot normally means that you have tied it correctly. Always pull knots up tightly while keeping the line moist (a little saliva works well) and check that they are tight. A knot that slips under pressure can cut the line. Bear in mind too that those knots requiring several turns around the standing line cannot be made with thick line as they drastically reduce the rated strength of the line.

Different knots are used for different purposes. Being able to tie good knots gives you all-round confidence, not only in your tackle but also in your ability to subdue and land a fish, so identify a couple of knots that are applicable to your type of fishing and learn to tie them well. Nothing gives the angler greater peace of mind, especially when fishing with light line, than knowing that his link with the fish has been made with line which is in good condition and that he has used the best knot and tied it well.

KNOTS FOR TYING ON HOOKS

Improved clinch knot
This is the simplest and most dependable knot with which to tie on a hook or a swivel.

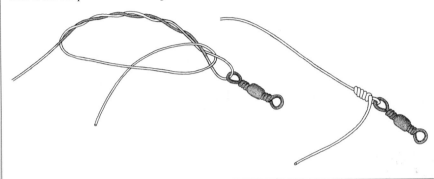

Palomar knot
An easy-to-tie knot that is very strong.

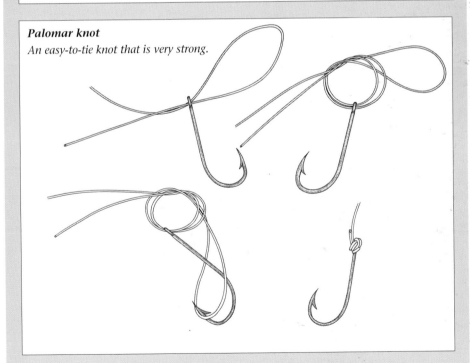

Common snell knot

Originally developed for hooks with flattened eyes, this knot is used chiefly on hooks with their eyes bent back or forward. It is strong and can in fact be used for any hook.

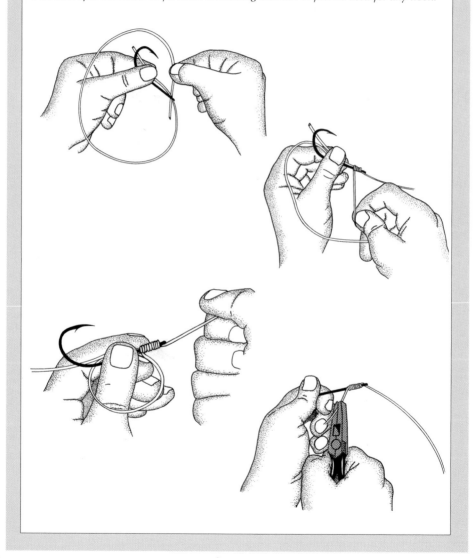

KNOTS FOR TYING LINE TO LINE AND LINE TO LEADER

Blood knot

This is the knot to use for joining lines of more or less similar diameter.

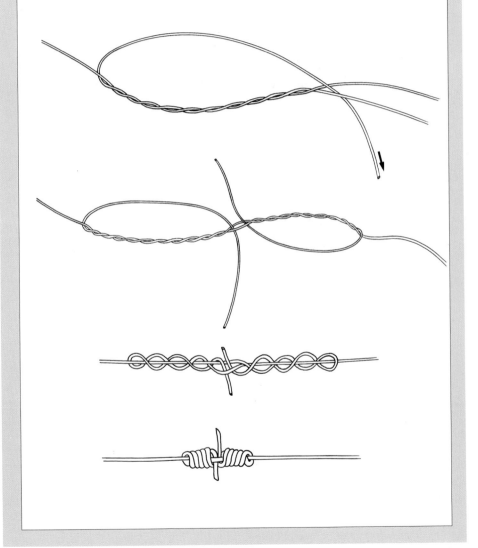

Surgeon's knot

This knot is suitable for tying leader to line, where the diameters vary considerably.

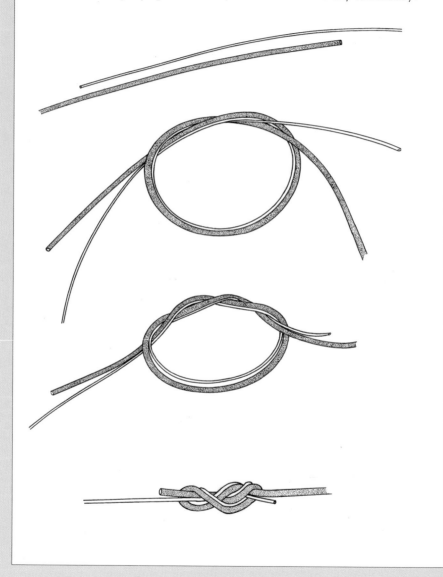

Albright knot

An ideal knot to tie when the diameter of the leader and that of the line are different. It is suitable for gamefishing when the leader is wound through the guides.

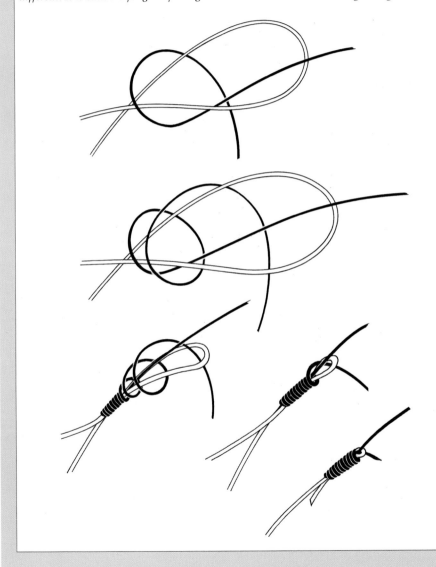

KNOTS FOR TYING DOUBLE LINES

Double lines are used mainly for offshore trolling. The double line provides extra strength and protection, especially when the fish is close to the boat or dives under the boat.

Bimini twist

This is probably the most popular knot used for making up a double line.

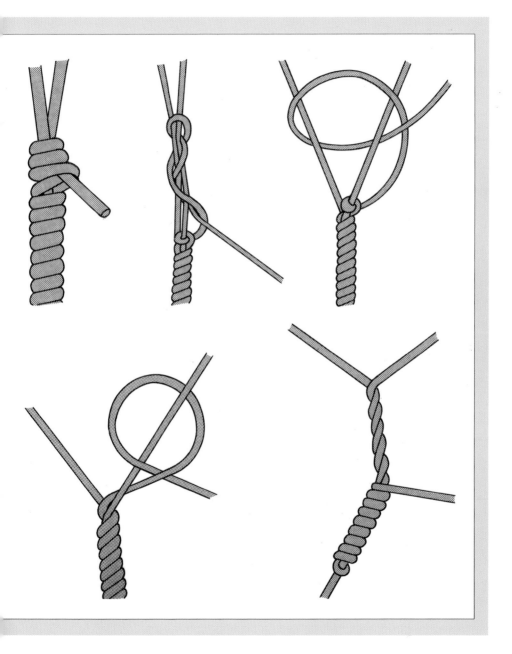

Spider hitch

A quick and easy knot to use to make up a double line.

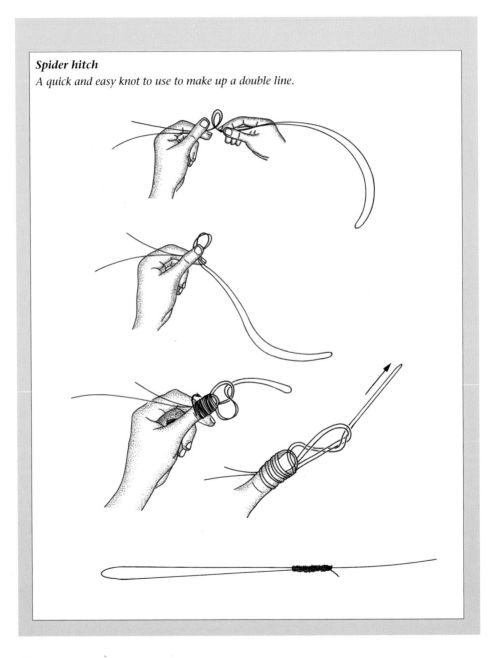

KNOT FOR TYING ON LURES

Harrison's loop knot

This knot is used to tie on a lure by means of a loop that will not impede the action of the lure.

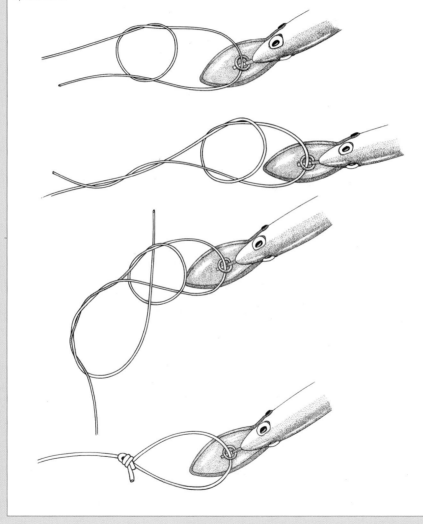

RIGS

The term 'rig' is used for the manner in which hooks and sinkers are tied on to present bait in the most attractive and natural way.

STANDARD ROCK FISHING RIG

This rig can be used with heavy or light tackle. The choice of tackle will depend on the state of the sea, and the mass of the sinker used will depend on how rough or calm conditions are. Always try to use as light a sinker as possible for the most natural presentation of the bait.

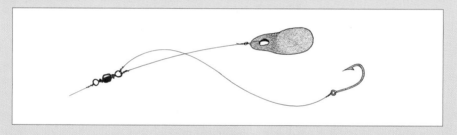

STANDARD RIG WITH SLIDING SINKER TRACE

This rig is normally fished with the sinker trace longer than the hook trace, as it makes casting easier. If conditions are calm or the fish are biting shyly, try lengthening the hook trace. A long hook trace will move more freely in the current and may entice a shy fish to grab the bait.

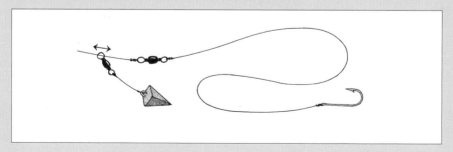

SLIDING SINKER RIG FOR SURF FISHING

This rig is particularly suitable for shad (elf) fishing. A grab sinker usually replaces the normal sinker, particularly in rough conditions, as it prevents tackle from being rolled around, tangling, or even washing ashore. (If the sea is calm it may be possible to fish with a normal sinker.) The hook trace has a small float to keep the bait off the sea bed, out of reach of crabs and bottom feeders. The float can be made from a wine-bottle cork or, if you are fishing in the southwestern Cape, from the float of a rock lobster ring net. (These sometimes wash up on the beach and are ideal to cut up for bait floats.) For shad, most anglers use a red float, as the fish seems to prefer this colour.

A short steel trace with a 10- to 15-kilogram breaking strain prevents bite-offs. If shad are reluctant to take the bait try fishing without the steel trace.

When fishing for kob, spotted grunter or bream it is best to fish without the float and steel trace, as these species forage on or near the bottom and are not capable of biting off the hook trace.

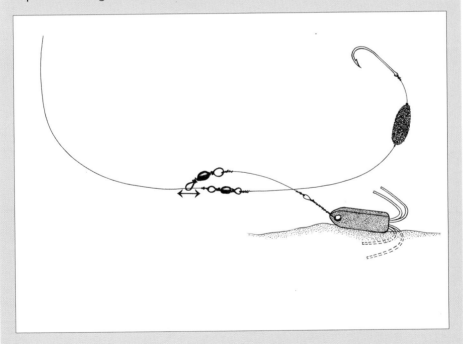

RUNNING SINKER RIG

This rig can be used when fishing from the shore or from a boat, and either with a swivel, which will keep the sinker away from the hook, or with the sinker running freely to the hook.

The running sinker rig is ideally used when fish are being finicky, as they feel very little resistance when they pick up the bait. It is essentially a light-tackle rig as the larger ball and barrel sinkers are likely to jam on the eye of the hook and also push down on the bait, spoiling the way in which it is presented.

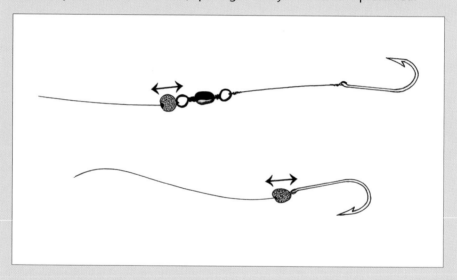

LIVE-BAIT RIGS

The type of rig you choose for fishing with a live bait depends on whether you are going to swim the bait from the shore or a boat, or whether you have to cast the bait some distance.

In the first case you could choose to use a float (see opposite left), the size of which will depend on the size of the bait, as live baits are normally aimed at pelagic or semi-pelagic species. A float therefore helps to keep the bait in the zone where the species is likely to feed.

If the live bait has to be cast in order to reach a specific hole or deeper water, the rig illustrated opposite (right) can be used.

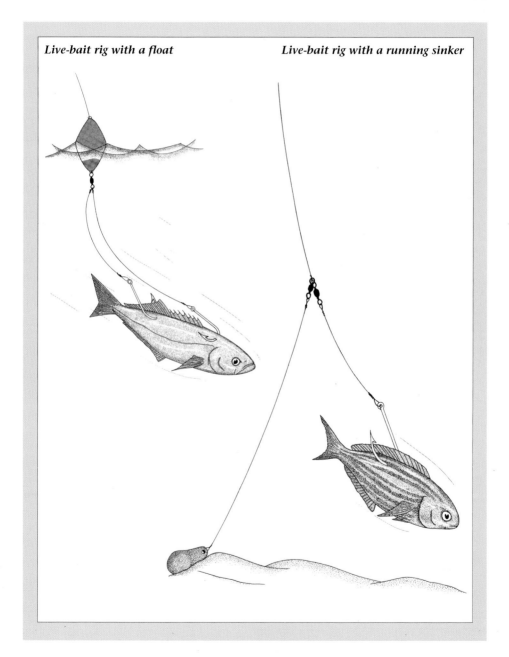

Live-bait rig with a float

Live-bait rig with a running sinker

CHAPTER FIVE

BAIT

A rock pool at low tide.

Most fish will readily take a bait that is fresh and attractively presented, and the best way of ensuring that your bait looks and smells as tempting as possible is to collect it yourself. Once collected, the bait must be looked after with care to maintain its fresh smell and appearance.

Many bait species, however, are inaccessible during normal tides and a special effort needs to be made to collect them over spring tides. As a result, anglers are often tempted to collect more than the legal bag limit – to the detriment of all, for as bait species become less abundant and more difficult to collect, the angler is obliged to travel further afield and venture out on more dangerous reefs. In addition, with their traditional feeding grounds depleted, the fish leave the area. The intertidal zone is particularly sensitive to over-exploitation and it is therefore the duty of each and every angler to play a responsible role in conserving resources.

The following rules are common sense and are not diffi-cult to observe. A little thought today can make all the difference to tomorrow's fishing:

1. Take only as much bait as you need for the day.
2. When you turn over rocks in your search for bait, make sure that you roll them back to their original positions so that all the organisms attached to the undersides are not disturbed and continue to live.
3. Take good care of your live bait so that whatever is not used can be returned to the water at the end of the day with a good chance of its surviving.
4. Never leave tins or packaging behind on the beach.

BAIT FOR SHORE AND INSHORE BOAT ANGLING

The angler fishing from the shore has a large variety of bait types which can be used for the species that feed among shallow reefs, sandy gullies or deep-water ledges of the nearshore zone. Collecting the bait for these species often involves going out on to exposed reefs some distance from the shore or climbing down a rock face to cut bait in a low tidal pool. When bait-collecting involves this, keep an eye on the water or have someone assist you and ask him to warn you of approaching waves.

If you are a stranger to an area, never go near the water without watching the sea for at least 10 to 15 minutes, especially where the water is very deep close to the side of a rock face or reef. In shallow water, waves are rolling in one after the other and are easily noticed. In deeper water the waves roll in less frequently and you may arrive at a spot that looks safe but in fact it may be washed by irregular waves. Every year people are washed off rocks by so-called 'freak' waves and drowned. Often these waves are part of a set of three or four waves which is followed by a fairly long period of calm water. The

The ideal spot for wonderworm.

inexperienced angler may not be aware of this pattern and can be trapped on a reef or ledge by a wave that appears seemingly out of nowhere. Spend sufficient time watching the water from a safe distance before venturing out on to the reefs; it may save your life.

BLACK MUSSELS

When inspecting the gut contents of fish caught among the rocks from the shore it is remarkable how many times the entire gut is filled with juvenile black mussels. Galjoen are particularly fond of small black mussels and may often be caught in a gully where the sand has been washed out and the newly exposed rocks are covered with freshly settled juvenile black mussels.

It is thus surprising that, despite the fact that they are easier to collect than redbait or white mussels, black mussels are not commonly used as bait. Mullet (harders) can be fished for by first crushing black mussels to make a 'chum', which is thrown into the water to attract the nearby fish, and then by throwing in a drift line with a small hook baited with a piece of mussel. This technique works very well at low tide in tidal pools or in open waters when the sea is calm.

Black mussels.

Black mussels can be picked by hand although a knife or a screwdriver is more convenient to use to sever the anchoring fibres. Remember not to exceed the bag limit (see page 226), and take home what is left at the end of the day, as black mussels make excellent eating. (Be sure to heed any red-tide warning.)

BLOODWORM

Bloodworms can be collected from Saldanha Bay to Durban in estuaries and on the sheltered sandy beaches of bays, where they live in U-shaped burrows, the surface of which resembles a small volcano. Bloodworms draw in water at one end of their body and pump it out the other, which is why at one end of the burrow there is a depression while the other end is raised.

Bloodworm is the favoured bait of white steenbras, and kob (kabeljou) but many other fish also find it irresistible. In addition, it has the advantage of being difficult to remove from the hook. Bloodworm is therefore worth whatever trouble it takes to obtain. It may be collected by using either a prawn pump or a length of wire with a barb on the end. The wire is fed down a hole until a bloodworm is felt and hooked. It cannot be pulled out of the burrow as the hook will tear through the flesh, so the sand has to be dug away while the tension is held on the wire – a method that requires a lot of practice.

Above: Pumping for bloodworm.
Below: A freshly collected bloodworm makes an excellent bait.

To collect bloodworms with a prawn pump, place the end of the pump over the hole and pump four or five times, emptying the contents on to the sand. (If the tide is pushing in, you will need a fine mesh bag, kept afloat by a small inner tube, through which each pump load is sifted.) If you are unsuccessful, probe the hole with your hand as sometimes the worm is lifted free of its burrow but not pumped out.

Bloodworms are filled with body fluid and sand when collected and must be cleaned before being used or stored. Nip off the thin tail part and squeeze out the body

contents by running the thumb and forefinger from the head downwards. Cleaned worms should be individually wrapped in clingwrap and stored in the freezer.

CORAL OR MUSSEL WORMS

Coral worms are found among the barnacles and mussels on exposed reefs from Port Nolloth to Port Elizabeth. Although a good bait, I am reluctant to recommend their use as collecting them often involves destroying large tracts of mussel or barnacle growth on the rocks exposed during low tide.

The worms can be kept on a bed of fine seaweed in a well-drained container, such as a bucket or tin with holes made in the bottom, and as long as they are occasionally sprayed with fresh sea water and kept in a cool place they will last for days.

CRABS

The large *red crabs* found in rock pools are highly sought after as bait for white musselcracker (brusher). Although they have a hard outer shell they are brittle and must be handled very carefully when placed on the hook. The best way of securing a crab to a hook is to tie it on with elastic

Sand crab.

cotton without passing the hook through the crab. In this way, the crab stays alive and a very natural-looking bait can be made up.

When collecting crabs, anglers exploit the fact that the octopus is a natural enemy of the crab. The angler attaches a large hook, such as a 10/0, to the end of a stick approximately 1,5 metres in length. (Better still is the thin end of a broken fishing rod.) He then cuts a piece of car inner tube, preferably red in colour, into four or more frills to resemble the tentacles of an octopus and binds this on to the shank of the hook. When this 'octopus' is pushed into crevices or under rocks the crabs try to escape by climbing out of the pool, where they can easily be collected. Be careful when picking them up as they can give you quite a nip: the safest method is to grab them across the back.

Crabs can be kept alive by storing them in a cool, damp container, and as long as their gill chambers are not allowed to become dry they will stay alive for some time.

The small *common shore crab* found in shallow rock pools can also be used as bait for bottom feeders such as galjoen and bream.

Mole crabs (sea lice) are not really crabs at all. These interesting creatures occur mainly in northern KwaZulu-Natal and there are fairly strict regulations controlling their capture. They are most easily caught at low tide on a flat stretch of beach. Wait for a wave to wash up and then subside and you will see – if there are mole crabs present – a number of Vs in the sand. These are the marks of mole crabs burrowing into the sand. Approach swiftly but do not tread heavily on the sand, and then dig behind the V until you feel the creature. Close your hand around it and slip it into your bait container.

Mole crabs will live for a long time in sea water and are fished most effectively when alive. They are excellent bait for those species, such as pompano, which feed close inshore, particularly where there are sandy beaches.

Mole crabs.

MUD PRAWNS, SAND PRAWNS AND CRACKER SHRIMPS

There are two species of burrowing prawns that abound in the mud or sand flats of most estuaries. They are the brownish-green mud prawn and its pink cousin, the sand prawn, which can be distinguished from the mud prawn by its single enlarged nipper. Sand prawns occur from Lambert's Bay to Delagoa Bay, mostly in estuaries, where the tidal flats are pockmarked with the entrances to their burrows. Mud prawns are messy to collect as they occur,

Sand prawns.

as their name implies, on muddy flats or under stones in estuaries. They range from the Olifants River estuary on the west coast to Delagoa Bay.

Another prawn, excellent as bait but more scarce, is the pistol or cracker shrimp (also called *skietkapper* by the gillies of Plettenberg Bay), which occurs from Still Bay eastwards as far as Mozambique.

Sand and mud prawns may be collected with purpose-built prawn pumps. The pump is placed over the opening of the burrow and pumped two or three times. When pumping at low tide on the dry flats, the pump load can be discharged on to the dry sand, but when pumping in ankle- to knee-deep water a fine-mesh floating sieve, similar to that used when collecting bloodworms, must be used. If you do not have a prawn pump, an empty jam tin, held upside down and forced down over the hole, should eject the prawn from its hole. This is a very messy way of collecting prawns, however, as the muddy water squirts up all over the place and even if you are wearing waders you end up dirty and wet.

Even more messy is the manner in which *cracker shrimps* are collected. They betray their presence in the weed beds of an estuary by the loud clicking noise they make: they use their enlarged nipper like a finger and thumb to make the clicking or snapping noise. Cracker shrimps are collected by marching on the spot, tramping up and down in one spot until a muddy pool is formed. The cracker shrimps rise to the surface to escape the muddy water and may then be collected at the edge of the pool. Cracker shrimps are not as soft as mud prawns or sand prawns and last much longer on the hook. They are excellent as bait for spotted and white steenbras as well as for river bream.

All burrowing prawns should be handled very carefully. Keep them in a container on a bed of fine seaweed which can be freshened up occasionally by splashing sea water over it. Don't put fresh, live prawns in stagnant water or store them with dead prawns, as this causes the live prawns to deteriorate.

A sand prawn rigged to present an attractive bait.

OCTOPUS

Octopus is a very versatile bait-type. It can be used from the shore to catch kob and poenskop (black musselcracker) and is also an excellent bait to use from the boat when fishing for 'red' fish such as red stumpnose, red roman and red steenbras. A strip of octopus leg is also an ideal bait for yellowtail.

Octopus.

Octopus can be found at low tide sheltering under rocks or in crevices in tidal pools. The same method used for catching crabs can be used for catching octopus.

To an octopus the tasselled strips of red inner tube (see page 79) look like a prey and the octopus will leave its shelter to grab the bait. Octopus normally capture their prey by wrapping their tentacles around it and so will become trapped by the hook hidden underneath the tassels.

Octopus stores extrememly well in a freezer. The tentacles can be cut off and either cleaned or left with the 'skin' on, and individually wrapped and frozen. To clean the tentacles, 'tenderize' the dead octopus by beating it against a smooth rock and then roll it in the sand in order to obtain a firm grip on the creature. Encircle one tentacle at a time with the thumb and forefinger and pull down towards the tip of the tentacle. The suckers, along with the slimy outer layer, will be stripped off.

Cleaned octopus – and squid – should always be white in colour. As soon as the flesh turns pink it is no longer fresh or attractive as a bait.

REDBAIT

Redbait is one of the most popular baits in the southwestern and southern Cape, where it is used to catch bottom feeders such as galjoen, blacktail (*dassie*), *wildeperd* (zebra) and even red roman. Redbait occurs from Saldanha Bay to Port Elizabeth and at places further along the eastern Cape coast, where it is found at low tide on rocky outcrops, in the rocky crevices of gullies, or on the side of ledges that are exposed to strong wave action. This bait is collected by cutting the flesh out of the pods, which may be either isolated or growing in large colonies.

Anglers identify two types of redbait. The first has olive green pods that stick out of the water at low tide, often seen along the rocks of the False Bay and southern Cape coastline as far as Port Elizabeth, as well as higher up the eastern Cape coast. These pods are large and the red flesh is thick, which makes it difficult to present as an enticing bait on the small hooks that are normally used with this type of bait.

The second type, often referred to as 'sand bait', is brownish in colour, and has a smaller, softer pod. Because it occurs in deep water it is usually collected from beaches along the southwestern and southern Cape coast after periods of rough seas. It is preferred by anglers, as the flesh is thinner and, though paler in colour, has a stronger smell and is more juicy and attractive on the hook.

An advantage of collecting this redbait is that the angler has time to select and cut bait out of the smaller pods without destroying a live colony. Sometimes, however, a very old and rotten pod may appear fresh but when you cut it open the smell, especially when the juice squirts all over you, is liable to keep your family and friends at a safe distance for days!

The reddish flesh of redbait is an ideal bait for most rock and surf species.

Some anglers prefer to 'ripen' redbait by burying the flesh in the sand or simply hanging it outdoors in a wicker basket. When fishing with ripe redbait the orange stains it leaves on clothes and the rotten smell may detract a little from the experience. No amount of scrubbing with soap and water takes the smell away; vanilla essence rubbed into the hands helps to disguise it somewhat.

Galjoen seem to prefer 'ripe' redbait; other species such as blacktail and *wildeperd* are often found feeding on pods that have been cut open and can be caught on a drift line as the tide rises. Commercial oyster-pickers along the southern Cape coast often attach to their belts a short length of thin nylon with a hook baited with redbait and in this way catch a variety of bottom feeders while standing waist-deep in water.

The accepted way of storing redbait today is to allow the cut flesh to drain for a day or two by hanging it in a tree in a wicker basket – away from the house – and then to pack the bait in a plastic screw-top jar and to store it in a deepfreeze. Make sure that the outside of the jar is clean and dry before putting it in the deepfreeze otherwise the smell of redbait will permeate other food stuffs and be unpleasant on opening the freezer. There are many methods of preserving redbait other than in a deepfreeze. They range from salting the bait or treating it with a mixture of salt and sugar, to treating it with boracic powder, draining the excess fluid and storing the bait in a jar in the fridge.

PRESERVING BAIT

Spread your bait on newspaper to draw off the excess fluid, then make up a mixture of one dessertspoonful of sugar to one cup of salt. Fill a glass jar with alternate layers of bait (cut in pieces if necessary) and the salt and sugar mixture, leaving about 3 to 4 centimetres of space at the top of the jar as the mixture will draw water.

ROCK LOBSTER

On the east coast poenskop love the white tail-meat of rock lobster, as do rockcod. It is also a favourite of seventy-fours, bronze bream and spotted grunter. On the west coast anglers use it on a thin hook trace to catch hottentot, and when rock lobster is in the soft shell stage, immediately after having shed its hard carapace, every fish in the sea is attracted to it.

Rock lobsters are found in caves and crevices, usually in fairly shallow water (ideally around 3 to 5 metres) and are frequently dived for. However, west coast nearshore boat anglers catch them by means of hoop nets.

To catch hottentot, small pieces of the tail meat are tied on to a hook with cotton. For larger fish, the hard shell is peeled off the tail-meat and the entire tail is tied on to the hook .

SQUID (CHOKKA)

Like white mussels, squid is a bait that can be used for many species. Bottom feeders, especially red roman, red stumpnose and kob, take squid readily, and a thin, long strip of squid is a very popular bait for yellowtail.

Squid is normally not caught from the shore but boat anglers make good catches along the coast and especially in the bays from False Bay to Port Alfred. Jeffreys Bay in the eastern Cape has become the centre of the squid-fishing industry and thousands of tons of squid are caught here each year by means of squid jigs on handlines. A wide selection of prawn-like squid jigs is available and, as with all lures, it is best to have a good range of shapes and colours in your tackle box.

The rig used to catch squid normally consists of a thin handline (with a 10- to 15-kilogram breaking strain) with a sinking jig tied to the end; the mass of the jig depends on the depth of the water and the strength of the current. One or two floating jigs can be fixed on short traces above the sinking jig.

Squid.

Squid can sometimes be seen on an echosounder. When a shoal is spotted the anchor should be dropped carefully and the squid lines lowered to within 1 or 2 metres of the sea bed, depending on the size of the swell and how rough or rocky the bottom is. The line should be tied at this depth to ensure that the jig reaches the same depth each time it is lowered. The movement of the boat, or the angler slowly moving the line up and down, attracts the squid to the jigs. There is no 'bite' as such; the angler must simply wait until he feels an additional weight on the line. Avoid jerking the line once a squid has been hooked as it falls off easily, and haul it up slowly and evenly. As a rule squid bite best at first light or late in the afternoon.

To clean squid remove the outer skin along with the fins and, if you want to keep the squid as a tube, loosen the transparent 'pen' and innards with the forefinger and then pull on the head to remove it. Wash the tubes in a bucket of clean sea water to remove all traces of black ink. The opaque or white flesh must be kept in a cool place on the boat. If enough squid has been caught for the angler to take some home, the tubes should be dried on absorbent paper and individually wrapped before storing in the deepfreeze.

SWIMMING PRAWNS

Many species of swimming prawns enter the estuaries of the east coast as part of their life cycle. These prawns are excellent to use as bait as they are favoured by most of the estuarine fish species, particularly kob, spotted grunter and white steenbras.

There are a number of ways in which swimming prawns can be collected. In the upper reaches of tidal rivers small prawns can be collected by dragging a piece of fine-mesh netting or a scoop net through the weed beds. At night the larger prawns swim on the surface and can be collected with a scoop net with the assistance of a powerful torch or lamp to spot them. Occasionally they are also caught incidentally in bait seine nets or in throw-nets.

Swimming prawns can be kept fresh and alive by placing them in fine weed in a well-drained container and keeping them moist and cool by occasionally splashing water over them.

VENUS EARS ('SIFFIE')

Venus ears are often mistaken for small perlemoen but are in fact a different species. They are found in rocky crevices at low tide from False Bay to Port St Johns. They are probably most sought after in the area from Cape Infanta to Cape Recife, where they are used as bait for white mussel-cracker (brusher). They are tough and resilient, keep for days without spoiling, and once on the hook will last all day. Although easy to collect it requires a trained eye to spot them as they are often well hidden among mussels and redbait pods.

WHITE OR SAND MUSSELS

White mussels can be used as bait for most species of fish, even, at times, shad (elf). I once fished at Boknesstrand on the Alexandria coast and was advised to bring along a few packets of pink prawn to fish for bronze bream. Pink prawn is a very good bait for bream but over a week's fishing holiday can become fairly expensive, so after this experience, I took some white mussels on my next visit and was happy to find that they worked just as well.

Jiving for white mussels.

White mussels occur at low tide on sandy beaches from Port Nolloth to Woody Cape east of Port Elizabeth. On the west coast larger mussels are found close to the spring low-tide level, while at Hermanus and beyond these mussels, regardless of their size, occupy a narrow band between the high- and low-water levels. This makes mussel-collecting on the south and east coasts easy in comparison with that on the west coast, where collectors often end up standing waist-deep in ice-cold water.

To collect white mussels on the west coast you have to teach yourself the 'mussel jive', a twisting motion of the lower body which gradually forces the feet under the sand until a mussel is felt. Where mussels are abundant this can be good fun as well as healthy exercise, but where mussels are scarce it ends up being plain hard work.

While white mussels are normally found about 15 centimetres under the sand, in some sheltered bays on the west coast, like Britannia Bay and Elandsbaai, the mussels bury themselves just beneath the surface of the sand and can be felt under foot when walking in the water.

A collecting bag, which can be purchased from a dive or sports shop, is ideal to wear around the waist when collecting mussels as it leaves both hands free to dig.

White mussels.

Wearing a wet suit, however, or at least a pair of wet-suit pants, is a must if you have to spend some time in cold water, but you cannot wear neoprene booties, as you have to be able to feel the mussels with your feet.

Along the beaches of the south and east coast, mussels can be located by walking along the water's edge and looking for siphon holes. Once found, the mussels are fairly easy to dig out as, unlike on the west coast, collectors are rarely disturbed by breaking waves and can sit comfortably on their haunches while digging with their hands.

Through the years many techniques of preserving white mussels have been used. As in the case of redbait, these techniques, such as salting or preserving in a mixture of salt and sugar, were probably necessary when deepfreeze space was either at a premium or not available: many of the old fishing shacks had no electricity so necessity became the mother of invention.

White mussels can be kept alive for days by storing them in a hessian sack and by dunking the sack in the sea for a short while each day. The only drawback to live mussels, as opposed to mussels that have been frozen, is that they are tough and difficult to tie on as a neat and attractive bait; the cotton tends to tear through the flesh and small fish are able to remove the flesh from the hook in a flash.

The most practical way to keep white mussels is to store them in a bag in the deepfreeze. To avoid their drying out make sure that they are well wrapped. In this way they can be stored for six months or longer. A defrosted white mussel makes a soft and attractive bait but should be tied on carefully as it easily overfills a 1/0 or even a 2/0 hook and can cover the tip of the hook.

WONDERWORMS

Wonderworms are found in the sand under rocks and boulders. They occur along the west coast, around the Cape and at least as far east as Port Alfred (whether they occur higher up on the east coast I have yet to determine). They are very good bait for bottom feeders that are caught from the shore but can be difficult to collect, as fairly large rocks and boulders have to be moved before you can start to dig.

The depth to which you have to dig depends on the depth at which you strike bedrock, for that is where you will find these worms. If you like your hands to be smooth and neat in appearance, with well-manicured nails, digging for wonderworms is something you should avoid: the coarse sand, grit and broken shells tear nails and cut fingertips – and just wait for the aching back muscles the next day.

Above: *Digging for wonderworm.*
Below: *Wonderworm on the hook.*

That said, wonderworms are well worth the effort put into collecting them, as they are an excellent bait, especially when the water is not very rough and the fish have been toying with all the other baits you have tried. If you happen to fish next to someone who is using wonderworm and you don't have any, you may as well move to another spot. It is very frustrating to watch an angler pulling out fish after fish while the fish play around with your bait without swallowing it.

The wonderworms you collect should be washed and salted soon after collecting and kept in a brine solution until you get home. Remove them from the brine and wrap them in newspaper or clingwrap before storing them in the deepfreeze.

SARDINES (PILCHARDS)

Sardines are used by all manner of shore and boat anglers. Sardines may be fished whole or cut up into strips or fillets, and because the flesh is very oily, this bait attracts fish far more quickly than other, more hardy baits, such as squid or octopus. A good bait to make up, especially when there are lots of small fish biting, is a strip of squid with a fillet of sardine added.

Sardines cut into small blocks are excellent for creating a 'chum slick' when fishing from a boat for species such as tuna or yellowtail. The sardines are cut into small pieces and thrown into the water at regular intervals until a shiny slick can be seen extending upwind from the boat. This slick and the chum itself can attract and hold an entire shoal, providing hours of hectic and exciting fishing.

Some anglers are in the fortunate position of being able to pack their own sardines during the sardine run, which takes place most years along the south coast of KwaZulu-Natal. The rest of us, however, have to rely on the frozen sardines supplied by the pelagic factories on the west coast. Sardines that have been freshly caught and frozen in small quantities in order to lower the core temperature quickly make the most attractive baits, especially where fishing for

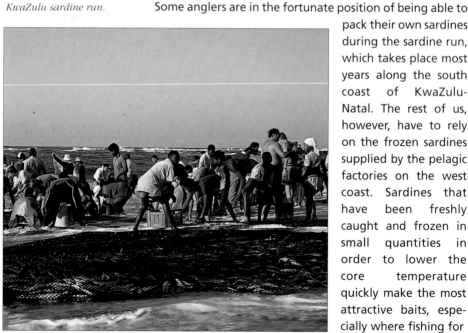

The excitement of the annual KwaZulu sardine run.

shad (elf) is concerned. Some of the factories have equipped their boats with special containers which they fill with an ice slurry to keep the sardines in the best possible condition while they are transported back to the factory, and these supply bait of a good quality. Other suppliers are not so careful and once the bait starts to defrost it often becomes so soft that it falls off when you cast.

Make sure that the sardine bait you buy is not yellow and that the skin does not have a crinkled appearance, as this signifies that the sardines are old, have probably been defrosted at least once and are no longer of any use as bait. Get to know who supplies the best bait.

LIVE BAIT FOR SHORE AND INSHORE FISHING

Fishing with live bait can be very exciting. Species such as kob, red steenbras, yellowtail, garrick and poenskop, to mention a few, are often taken on live bait.

Small fish, such as mackerel, *maasbanker*, pinky and karanteen, can be caught from a boat using a small baited hook on a drift line or a line weighted with a small sinker. Another way of catching bait fish is with a Yò-Zuri rig – a series of small lures that are jigged up and down. It is amazing to see the variety of fish taken by this method. Small live bait can be kept in a large bucket which is regularly replenished with fresh sea water. Battery-operated air pumps are available and if you are going to use live bait on a regular basis it is worth purchasing one.

Fishing for live bait from the shore can be just as much fun. A variety of small fish can be caught from harbour walls or in gullies from the rocks, while the beach or estuary angler will use a throw-net to catch his bait (normally mullet). This method is not as difficult to master as it may first appear and by following the steps illustrated overleaf, the technique can soon be acquired.

A number of sardines as bait: 1. Whole bait. 2. Split as snoek bait. 3. & 4. Typical shad baits. 5. Tail bait and chum for tuna.

PREPARING AND CASTING A THROW NET

1.

2.

*1. Lay out the net and check that the draw or purse lines are not tangled. **2.** Attach the throw line to your right wrist; coil the rest of the rope and hold it in the same hand. **3.** With the left hand grab the net about one third from the crown (the centre of the net when laid in a circle), coil once and transfer to the right hand. With the left hand pick up the lead line. **4.** Place three coils of lead line in the right hand.*

3.

4.

5.

6.

7.

5. Pick up the lead line so that half of the remaining line stretches between your right and left hand and the other half hangs clear.
6. Place your weight on your left foot and swivel around from the right. 7. Release the net as the right arm is pointing in the direction in which you are throwing the net. Release the net from both hands at the same time!
8. In ideal conditions the net should spread and land evenly. At first this will be difficult to achieve. However, you will still catch enough bait even if the net does not spread fully.

8.

DEEP-SEA ANGLING BAIT

The huge differences in technique, tackle and trace used by the shore angler as opposed to the deep-sea angler is further emphasized by the baits that are used. When deep-sea angling, the bait is not subject to the currents and moving waters of the surf zone. Trolled slowly behind a boat, the gentle forward motion of the bait can be harnessed into giving it an exciting action in the water. A bait rigged for slow trolling will also be very effective on the anchor or on the drift as the current can provide the movement required to give the bait a lifelike appearance.

GAMEFISHING IN KWAZULU-NATAL

While mullet, sardines, Japanese mackerel, pinky and skipjack (bonito) are popular gamefish bait in both KwaZulu-Natal and the Cape, the following fish are particularly favoured in KwaZulu-Natal, rigged with the 'couta trace. (See page 147.)

SHAD

Big baits, big fish. That maxim is especially true of big shad – a premier offering for the 'couta or giant kingfish, and look out for the billfish that takes a liking to the shad's shiny skin. Shad are caught in KwaZulu-Natal chiefly in the winter months and in the southern and south-western Cape from approximately December to May. (See page 115.)

SILKIE

Silkie or wolfherring is regarded as one of the KwaZulu-Natal 'superbaits'. It is caught by trolling small feathers along the back-line in much the same way as you would when fishing for queen mackerel (Natal snoek). Silkies are not commonly caught, and the best place to find them is in the catches of the seine netters who operate from Vetchie's Pier in Durban. Their catches are often sprinkled with a few silkies and also some walla-wallas. However, these fishermen net very early and only when conditions are ideal.

Opposite: Marlin, among the largest fish in the sea, are caught on slow-trolled live or dead baits.
Left: Silkie.

WALLA-WALLA

An excellent bait for gamefishing in KwaZulu-Natal is the walla-walla or ribbonfish. This bait can be caught along the back-line in dirty water, but almost always as a

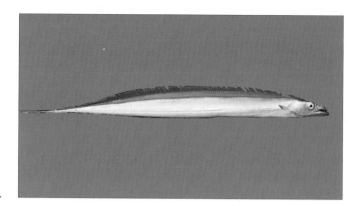

Walla-walla.

fluke, as its thin ribbon-like shape (at maturity it can measure a metre in length, yet only weigh 500 grams) makes it impossible to detect on an echosounder, nor does it stay in one spot for long. One place, though, where walla-walla can be found fairly consistently is in Durban harbour.

To spend an evening fishing for these wily fish is an adventure in itself. Slivers of sardine are tied with cotton on to a trace comprising a 1/0 long-shank hook and some heavy nylon, as walla-walla have incredibly sharp teeth and strong jaws. Fish with bass tackle or light bait tackle, as the key to successful fishing for this species is in detecting and winning the strike. Mysterious in the way it feeds, a gentle pull is felt as the walla-walla takes hold of the bait and then sinks as it swallows. Let it fade away and swim off a little way, then strike quite hard, as this fish has a bony jaw. Be assured that a success ratio of one to five is good going, and you can congratulate yourself if you take three of this species in an evening.

You might wonder why all the trouble for this bait, but you will soon be convinced that every walla-walla in the water will yield a strike – most likely from a 'couta, but there is also a good chance of an encounter with a billfish. Walla-walla are usually fished whole and dead, as many anglers say that when fished live they camouflage themselves too well.

Although mullet and skipjack are good ski-boat baits they are difficult to get to 'swim' without spinning, particularly when trolled, unless they are fished live.

A few bottomfish are also used as bait for gamefishing in KwaZulu-Natal, remembering that Sparidae (redfish) form a big part of the pelagic species' diet. Favourites include slinger, pimkles and scavengers, all readily caught at a depth of around 10 to 20 metres.

A windless day off Durban may be ideal boating weather but for fishing the angler will probably need to apply different strategies, as fish are often reluctant to bite or strike when the sea is calm.

CHAPTER SIX

ROCK AND SURF ANGLING

Casting with a Scarborough reel. It looks so simple when handled by an expert!

One of the attractions of rock and surf angling is the splendid scenery that is a backdrop to many of the fishing spots along the Cape and KwaZulu-Natal coasts. Alone or with a buddy on an isolated stretch of beach, with the sound of the surging waves breaking over rocks or on to the shore – such a place is all that is necessary to forget about the pressures and hassles of the working week or year.

The main attraction, of course, is the fish that can be caught, and the South African coastline offers an exciting variety.

Galjoen and many of the bream species are caught fairly close inshore, their specially adapted tails enabling them to forage in the turbid waters of the surf zone or among reefs; kob and shad, as well as several shark species, are caught by anchoring the bait just off the bottom; and still other species are fished for in gullies and holes using ultra-light tackle for maximum entertainment.

This chapter discusses the techniques and tackle required for some of the more popular shore angling species.

BRONZE BREAM
(Pachymetopon grande)

Other common names (though not officially recognized): John Brown (not to be confused with the blue-eyed Jan Bruin, which has a similar range but is not as plentiful), bluefish, das and, in the southern Cape, *pens-en-derm* because if its sizeable gut and entrails.

DISTRIBUTION
Bronze bream inhabit shallow, rocky coastlines and are found from Cape Agulhas up into Mozambique. From Port Elizabeth and beyond you may come across bronze bream in a shoal and if you are lucky you could end up with three or more. In KwaZulu-Natal and the eastern Cape they swim mainly in shallow water but can also be found in water as deep as 20 metres, and often shoaling with such fish as knifejaw, baardman and stone bream.

The hot spot for bronze bream is the KwaZulu-Natal south coast, where they spawn. There, mature specimens have been recorded at 40 to 45 centimetres in length. Along the southern Cape coast only the odd bronze bream is caught, often when fishing with redbait for galjoen.

FEEDING HABITS
Because they feed in shallow water, bronze bream are particularly sensitive to changes in water conditions and temperature and go off the bite very quickly. Their natural diet is the

algal plants that grow in turbulent water, which is the reason for their sharp, cutting jaws. The tiny crustaceans that occur on the algae also form part of their diet

BAIT

Owing to their natural vegetarian diet, bronze bream do not take bait as readily as some other bottom-feeding species. They will, however, take a soft bait such as pink prawn, rock lobster, or white mussel if it is well presented. Once hooked, this species provides good sport.

WHERE TO CATCH

At home in the shallows, bronze bream may be caught in conditions similar to those favoured by galjoen. Because they feed on rocky shelves, spring low tide is the best time to fish for this species. Good catches can often be made at this time by fishing the reefs that are out of reach during normal tides.

TACKLE AND TACTICS

At most of the spots where bronze bream are the target species, a fairly long cast is required. A 3,5-metre rod or even the standard beach rod (4 metres or longer) can be used, together with a reel filled with 12- or 14-kilogram breaking-strain nylon. Bronze bream have small mouths, and a 1/0 or 2/0 hook with a sliding sinker rig may improve your chances of outwitting them, as it will allow the fish to mouth the bait without feeling any resistance. A piece of bait on a thin hook trace will appeal far more than a chunk of bait anchored on the bottom.

THE HOOK-UP

Although one of the most common panfish along the Cape east coast, the bronze bream can be crafty and difficult to catch on occasions. It can take the bait with a heavy tug when on the bite but it is often very trying, as it is quite capable of toying with the bait – and cleaning the hook in the process – without giving the angler the slightest opportunity of setting the hook. Sometimes an angler may sense that something is mouthing the bait without feeling any resistance or movement on the line. In these cases, try to set the hook when you feel a tugging on the bait or when you feel your line becoming 'weightless'. Although this has been known to work, be prepared still to miss a few fish. The good news is that the more you fish for bronze bream, the better you become at sensing when to strike.

EATING QUALITY

The flesh of the bronze bream is very white and, despite being fatty, quite tasty to eat.

GALJOEN
(Coracinus capensis)

Other common names: damba, black-fish, black bream.

DISTRIBUTION

The galjoen, which occurs only in southern African waters and is South Africa's national fish, is one of the most sought-after angling species, especially along the western and south-western Cape coastline. In this region it reaches prime condition between May and August; along the southern and eastern Cape coasts and as far as Durban the prime months are September and October.

FEEDING HABITS

Galjoen feed close inshore, in gullies among reefs and redbait pods, in kelp beds and in freshly scoured holes on sandy beaches. They usually congregate in small shoals and tend to feed best on the incoming tide or at high tide in the churned-up, foamy water, and often at depths of less than one metre. Fishing conditions for galjoen are best when the waves break some distance offshore and white foamy water continuously rushes in. Avoid fishing on days when the water is calm and clear.

BAIT

If the stomach contents of a galjoen are examined, small black mussels and, to a lesser extent, fine weeds and small crustaceans will be found to predominate. The best bait to use for this species, however, are redbait (the ideal variety is the sand bait that washes up on beaches between Melkbosstrand on the west coast and Struisbaai on the southern Cape coast), white (sand) mussels, wonderworms, coral worms and small crabs. Redbait and white mussels are the most commonly used baits in the Cape and, while galjoen feed readily on frozen white mussels, they often prefer redbait that has been aged either by leaving it in a basket to drain or by burying strings of it in moist beach sand for two or three days. In KwaZulu-Natal, where there is a scarcity of redbait, galjoen can be taken on prawn or rock lobster.

WHERE TO CATCH

In certain places, such as Cape Agulhas, the nearshore area is very shallow and large expanses of the intertidal zone are exposed at low tide, and especially at spring low tide. Local fishermen take this opportunity to fish in holes and gullies that are normally out of reach and often good catches are made in this way. This form of angling can be dangerous, however, as the sea very quickly covers shallow reefs and boulders as the tide rises. The novice – or even the experienced angler who does not have a good knowledge of the area – can easily be left stranded on a reef some distance from the shore.

When fishing for galjoen you must cast as close to a reef or rocky outcrop as possible. In a gully you can normally identify the deeper water around a rock by the colour of the water, the absence of sand in suspension, or the fact that a swell passing through does not break in the deeper part of the gully. Cast your bait into this deeper water but as close to the rock as possible.

TACKLE AND TACTICS

The tackle selection for galjoen depends on the type of terrain in which you choose to fish. The different terrains can roughly be categorized as reefs and rocky gullies, high cliffs, or sandy beaches with outcrops of rocks.

Gully fishing Expert light-tackle anglers use short, quick-tapering rods, normally no longer than 2,5 metres, with a matching reel and 6- or 8-kilogram breaking-strain nylon. This is rigged with a small ball sinker, the mass of which will depend on how rough the water is, and a 1/0 or no. 1 hook. This type of 'skinny' tackle is suitable for use in terrain where the fish can be beached rather than having to be lifted out of the water.

The novice or occasional angler should use a quick-tapering fibreglass or graphite rod, 3,2-metres long, with a matching reel such as a

Shimano 20/40, Penn 500 or 501 or the Daiwa SL 50SH. It is best to use nylon with a 12- or 14-kilogram breaking strain but make sure that the line you use for the hook and sinker traces is thinner to ensure that your traces break off at the swivel if the line becomes stuck.

The mass of the sinker depends on the sea conditions and also on the class of the tackle you use; the rod and reel mentioned above would be classed as medium tackle and the mass of the sinker suited to this would be 5, 113 and 141 grams (3,5 and 5 ounces). Hook sizes also vary but a no. 1, 1/0 or 2/0 short shank or long shank are most often used, as galjoen has a small mouth. The hook and sinker traces can be rigged on a single swivel or on two swivels as a sliding rig.

Fishing from high cliffs into deep water Along the Mossel Bay, George, Knysna and former Transkei coast-lines, it is best to use a stiffer, longer rod, not only to lift the galjoen out of the water but also because you stand a good chance of hooking larger species such as white musselcracker (brusher or silver steenbras) and poenskop (black musselcracker). A 3,8-metre rod used with a reel which has a line capacity of 200 to 250 metres and a breaking strain of 16 kilograms would be ideal. In those circumstances I prefer to use a

An ideal spot for galjoen.

thicker hook trace (with a breaking strain of at least 18 kilograms), as you need more than your fair share of luck to land a white musselcracker or poenskop on the thinner traces normally used for galjoen.

A novel way of fishing for galjoen and other reef species from a high cliff is to reverse the hook and sinker sliding rig. Normally, when fishing with a sliding rig the hook trace is secured to a swivel, which in turn is attached to the main line. The sinker trace slides freely on the main line on its own swivel. When fishing from high cliffs into deep water, however – especially when the sea is calm – good catches can be made by reversing the above rig – that is, by attaching the sinker trace to the main line and allowing the hook trace to slide. In this way, when you cast into a gully, the sinker takes the main line into the mouth of the gully, while the baited hook trace enters the water last and sinks slowly. The bait floats freely and is snapped up by feeding fish. The strike is spectacular because the fish feels no resistance and rushes off.

Fishing from a beach with reefs or clumps of rocks some distance from the shore In this situation your tackle depends entirely on the length of cast required. If there are scoured-out holes or rocky outcrops close inshore, the shorter rod described above may be used. If a long cast is required, it might be better to resort to the longer (and therefore heavier) graphite or fibreglass beach rods (anything up to 4,5 metres in length). My personal preference, however, is the lighter graphite rod as the longer beach rods become quite heavy as the day wears on.

THE HOOK-UP

The bite of a galjoen can vary from a violent grab, normally in rough and foamy conditions, to endless toying with the bait in calmer clear water. When the water is calm but still has enough colour to keep the galjoen on the bite, a good idea is to double the length of the hook trace. The longer hook trace allows the bait to move around more freely in the current, often enticing the galjoen to grab it. Leave sufficient slack on the main line to allow the fish to bite without feeling any resistance. Be patient. Do not anticipate when the fish is going to take; give him time to bite firmly or even to pull your rod tip down.

The galjoen is a strong fighter for its size, even in the shallows, and you will have to take care when landing this fish. Its powerful tail helps it to use the waves and turbulent water to resist the effort of the angler winding it in. Take your time and do not force the fish, as you are likely to pull the hook out. When standing close to or in the water, lead the fish to the shore, avoiding reefs and rocks, and use the swell to slide the fish out. Fewer fish will be lost this way, as the hook often pulls out when the fish is lifted out of the water.

Once you have landed a galjoen, check that it is above the legal minimum total length of 35 centimetres and then despatch it by cutting through the gills. This kills the fish instantly and ensures that it bleeds, thereby enhancing the taste.

EATING QUALITY

The flesh of galjoen has a bluish tinge and, although for some it is an acquired taste, galjoen makes excellent eating provided that the fish is fat. (Lean galjoen have a rather gamey taste and I prefer to return these specimens to the sea.)

To test whether the fish you have landed is fat or thin, simply push together the two pelvic fins (those under the belly of the fish); if they extend beyond the anal opening, the fish is too thin, but if they don't reach the anal opening then you have landed a fat galjoen that will be ideal to cook on the braai.

GARRICK
(Lichia amia)

Other common name: leervis.

If ever there was an ideal species for young or inexperienced anglers to be introduced to gamefishing, garrick is the one. It gives the angler a more than fair chance to land it yet, unlike gamefishing from a boat, it does not cost a fortune to catch. What could be more relaxing than taking a young angler to a lagoon or river mouth, baiting up with a live bait and then sitting back to wait for the fish to strike? Unfortunately, most of the garrick caught in lagoons and estuaries are undersized and must be returned to the water, but the catching is fun and it introduces newcomers to the sport and to the importance of conservation.

DISTRIBUTION

Garrick occur from the Cape to KwaZulu-Natal, with a few catches having been recorded on the west coast. They are caught along the coast from False Bay to Delagoa Bay during the spring and summer months; thereafter they migrate to KwaZulu-Natal waters to spawn.

FEEDING HABITS

A predatory species, garrick feeds on shad (elf), mullet, pinky, sardine, karanteen and even the common blacktail. It is a spectacular surface feeder and many an estuarine angler has been startled by a sudden rush of garrick feeding on mullet in the shallows, as have ski-boat anglers fishing beyond the surf back-line of beaches. In the open ocean garrick usually stick close to the shore, near or just beyond the line of the waves breaking on the shore, where the pinkies or karanteen may be feeding or a shoal of mullet may be passing by.

BAIT

Live bait is the ideal means of catching garrick and any of the bait species mentioned above can be used. Strips of shad (elf) and skipjack (bonito) also work well. Catching a live bait, however, can sometimes be a problem because when garrick are biting well you normally find that mullet and other small fish simply disappear! Normally a light line and a small hook on a float is sufficient to catch a couple of karanteen or mullet, but the most effective way is to use a throw or cast net (see chapter 5) in a tidal river or into the surf.

WHERE TO CATCH

Prior to 1960 garrick were frequently caught in False Bay; today only an occasional catch is made and then usually in the Sandvlei lagoon or at Melkbaai near the Strand. These juvenile fish, however, are usually smaller than the legal size limit of 70 centimetres and many anglers prefer to release, or to tag and release, the specimens they catch – a practice that should be followed by all.

A nearshore species, garrick occur in small shoals beyond the surf back-line and close to rocky headlands of bays such as Robberg at Plettenberg Bay and Fransmanshoek near Mossel Bay. They are also found in lagoons and estuaries, often becoming trapped when river mouths silt up.

In winter garrick patrol the eastern coast of South Africa in shoals of between 20 and 50 fish. Spear-fishermen report seeing these shoals moving fast in and out of bays, running up and down points in search of their favourite foods. As the season progresses the shoals tend to break up and the fish swim in breeding pairs, or groups of three or four. After spawning – which, before their silting up, used to take place in KwaZulu-Natal's several huge open rivers and lagoons but now is limited to St Lucia and Durban harbour – the fish are ravenous and feed voraciously. This is when anglers in KwaZulu-Natal make their best catches. It is also about this time that the sardines (pilchards) make their appearance to the excitement of anglers.

In KwaZulu-Natal, hot spots are the mouths of those rivers where the garrick would like to enter to spawn, as well as long, rocky points which allow for calmer conditions in the bay.

Large garrick are often caught behind the back-line on live bait or spoons.

TACKLE AND TACTICS

Fishing from rocks or the beach This requires a sturdy rod of about 3,5 metres in length. In order to cast a large live bait or a lure from high rocks it is necessary to use nylon with a breaking strain of 12 or 14 kilograms on a reel that has a line capacity of 300 metres. A sliding sinker rig, similar to that used for shad, works well, or a ball or barrel sinker can be employed immediately above the swivel linking the hook trace to the main line. The choice depends largely on fishing conditions and the distance you have to cast. When fishing from a rocky point or reef and when the wind and current are favourable, it is possible to use a float.

Fishing with live bait As with all fish that are big or take a lot of line, it is important when fishing for garrick with live bait to have a reel with a smooth drag and to pre-set the drag tension accurately. Considering the long time that you may have to wait for a strike, having your tackle

An 18-kilogram garrick caught at Umzimkulu.

correctly set up is the least you can do to make sure that you will land the fish once you have hooked it.

The live bait can be rigged on a single hook, the size of which will depend on the size of the bait but can be anything from a 3/0 to a 7/0. Some anglers prefer to insert the hook in front of the first ray of the dorsal fin of their live bait, while others prefer to put it behind the fin – either way works well. Treble hooks can also be used but care must be taken to match the size of the treble to that of the bait.

It is not necessary to use a steel wire trace for garrick although it is advisable to use a strong nylon trace when fishing with a big live bait, as you never know what may ultimately grab the bait. For light-tackle fishing in estuaries and lagoons, a hook trace as light as 12 or 15 kilograms may be used, depending on the size of the bait, the breaking strain of the line and the size of the garrick you expect to catch in that particular stretch of water.

Fishing with spinner, plug or fly Using any of these lure-types is probably the most exciting way in which to catch garrick. Once again, the tackle depends on the terrain. When spinner- or plug-fishing from a headland, a quick-tapering 3,5-metre rod and a reel with a retrieval rate of higher than 5:1 and filled with 12- or 14-kilogram nylon should be used. Most anglers use a trace or leader of heavier breaking-strain line to prevent the rasp-like teeth of the garrick wearing through the line. When garrick are reluctant to strike, it may be necessary to tie the spinner or plug directly to the thinner main line; when all else fails, the latter is sometimes the only way to persuade them to have a go at the lure.

How fast or slowly the spinner or plug is retrieved and what action you impart to the lure by moving the rod depend on the fishing conditions at the time. The wily garrick spinner-man will try different retrieval rates, pointing the tip of the rod down or holding it up high, or even jerking the rod, when fishing with a plug. Even the most experienced angler becomes excited when a fish chases his plug or spinner and may end up retrieving too fast. Winding too fast, especially when you are standing on a high point, lifts the spinner and speeds it up as it moves closer to the rocks, which will ultimately result in the spinner bouncing along on the surface at such a rate that the fish cannot catch it. Always watch the action of your spinner and the behaviour of the fish, and adjust your technique accordingly.

The above holds true for spinning or plug fishing in the protected waters of an estuary, whether from the shore or from a boat. The only difference is that the angler may choose to fish with lighter tackle – as light as 4-kilogram line – provided the tackle is balanced. There are excellent fixed-spool reels on the market, and if used with a graphite rod matched to the reel, this ultra-light tackle is capable of landing surprisingly large fish.

Fine large specimens are often caught from a boat by trolling baits or lures behind the surf back-line close to the break-zone where garrick patrol, but this can be dangerous unless everyone on board is alert and watching for the larger waves that may appear to seawards.

THE HOOK-UP

In the words of Leo Biden: 'Garrick as a game fish is known as the "gentleman fighter", hardly ever resorting to dirty tricks like diving into a reef or cutting you off on a pinnacle. It tends to remain on the surface for the duration of the fight ...'

When fishing with a live bait, an increase in the swimming activity can be felt when a predator approaches the boat. At that stage your reel should be in free-spool, allowing the garrick to pick up and swallow the bait without feeling any

tension on the line. Once the garrick is moving away with the bait, slowly count to ten, lowering the rod tip at the same time. As soon as the rod tip is facing the direction in which the fish is swimming, engage the clutch and allow the fish to take up the tension in the line before you lift the rod. At this stage the bait should have been swallowed and lifting the rod will set the hook.

EATING QUALITY
Opinions on the quality of the flesh of garrick vary from place to place. However, the flesh of the smaller, legal-sized garrick is always good and can be smoked or fried.

KOB
(Argyrosomus hololepidotus)

Other common names: *kabeljou* and daga.

Few fish are known by such a variety of names as is the kob. While *kabeljou* is the favoured name along the west coast and is also the most frequently used alternative name, in Still Bay and Mossel Bay large kob are referred to as *boerkabeljou* and *kwagga* respectively. At Knysna and Plettenberg Bay they become *rietbulle*, and along the east coast and in KwaZulu-Natal they are sometimes referred to as salmon and the bigger specimens as daga or daga salmon.

DISTRIBUTION

Kob is widely distributed along the entire coast of South Africa, from the west coast right around to Mozambique and beyond. Because kob is a shoal fish, like shad (elf), it is one of the few remaining species that can be caught in fair quantities when it comes on the bite. When the shad or kob run is on, anglers can expect to catch one or the other for a number of days, provided conditions remain constant.

FEEDING HABITS

Kob are normally caught in the discoloured 'ginger beer' water where they depend to a large extent on their sense of smell to find the small fish and crustaceans on which they feed. They are found on the bottom, close to reefs, or in the holes and channels that wash open on sandy beaches. The quieter waters of river mouths and lagoons are also good places to fish for this species, especially at night.

BAIT

Kob prefer soft fish baits such as sardine (pilchard) and mackerel but will readily take a strip of squid, a leg of octopus, prawn or bloodworm, and in KwaZulu-Natal small whole shad or shad belly is commonly used. Generally, the bigger the bait, the bigger the kob you should catch.

WHERE TO CATCH

Kob is probably the best-known summer angling fish of the Cape and is especially common from False Bay along the southern Cape coast as far as Mossel Bay. In KwaZulu-Natal waters, on the other hand, the best catches are made during the winter months. The Aliwal Shoal and a wreck off Umdloti, north of Durban, are highly productive spots but good catches are reported along most of the KwaZulu-Natal coast.

Kob prefer sandy beaches and bays. They also provide excellent sport in river mouths as well as several kilometres upstream in tidal rivers. (In the Breede River kob have been caught as far away from the river mouth as Malgas.) They are caught in holes in rivers normally from one to two hours before high tide (river high tide, that is) and one to two hours after.

Because of the tidal action, it is best to fish from a boat. When there is no wind and the current is not strong, the boat can be anchored fore and aft across the tidal flow to provide a wide spread of baits, especially when two or more people are fishing.

TACKLE AND TACTICS

In places such as St Lucia in KwaZulu-Natal and in the larger tidal rivers of the Cape, such as the Breede, shore and boat anglers often use two rods when fishing for kob. One line is baited with a bloodworm and fished from a rod holder, while a rod carrying a live bait is held in the hand so that the angler can free-spool the line when the bait is taken. Squid is particularly good to use from a boat in deeper waters where there is a greater likelihood of 'peckers' finishing the bait before a decent-sized kob comes near it.

The tackle used for kob fishing depends on the terrain.

Shore fishing When fishing from the beach it is best to use a 4- or 4,5-metre surf rod with a heavy tip, as it is quite often necessary to cast a big bait as well as a heavy sinker (a 5- or 6-ounce) a long distance. In the Cape anglers prefer to use a multiplying reel filled with 12- to 17-kilogram breaking-strain line. In KwaZulu-Natal the Scarborough centre-pin reel still remains popular with surf anglers.

When fishing from the rocks the rod can be shorter – especially if there are obstructions behind you that make it difficult to use a longer rod – but it should still be sturdy and capable of casting the bigger, heavier kob baits.

A whole or cut sardine bait rigged on a large hook such as an 8/0 Kendall round and fished with a sliding sinker trace is one of the most

A good-sized kob – one of surf-fishing's top prizes.

common rigs used. Fishing off the beach with a live mullet (harder) into a deep hole will often produce very good results, especially when small fish or 'peckers' are ripping your soft cut-baits apart. A sliding sinker trace or a ball or barrel sinker, which slides freely on the main line above the swivel, can be used.

One or two hours before and during high tide are usually the best times to fish for kob from the shore. When the wind blows onshore or along the coast (longshore) and the water takes on that light brown, ginger beer colour, reasonable catches can be made during daylight hours. However, kob are known to bite best just before sunrise and at dusk. The persevering angler who is prepared to put in the hours and fish throughout the night produces consistent results and has the best chance of landing that once-in-a-lifetime catch. Boat anglers fishing in bays or in estuaries can vouch for the many cold and unpleasant nights they have spent fishing for kob but can also produce photographs to prove the many excellent catches they have made in doing so.

River, lagoon or bay fishing These areas probably provide the most spectacular sport for light-tackle kob-fishing enthusiasts. Because kob are not strong fighters, surprisingly large specimens can be landed on light tackle when the angler is fishing away from reefs or can follow the fish in a boat if necessary. A short boat rod and a reel that has a smooth drag and has a line capacity of 200 to 300 metres would be ideal. A fixed-spool reel can be used but you may end up without enough line should you not be able to follow the fish. Nylon with a breaking strain of 8 kilograms (or even less) would be sufficient for even the novice angler to land a fish of which he could be proud.

When fishing in rivers or bays, the mass of the sinker – or whether a sinker is necessary at all – depends on how calm conditions are and the strength of the current. Under ideal circumstances a light sliding sinker can be used with live bait or cut bait, or it may even be possible to swim the live bait without a sinker or to use a whole sardine as a drift bait.

When fishing in a river or in the open sea, kob may also be caught near the bottom. A line baited with a whole sardine, a cut-bait or a piece of squid and a fillet of sardine works well, lowered to within a metre or two of the sea bed. It is best to lower the bait to the bottom and then wind the line back up a metre or two to keep the bait off the bottom where the smaller sharks and rays may not be such a nuisance. However, there are occasions when kob go off the bite and you have to fish hard on the bottom and put up with catching some of the less attractive species, such as barbel. Conversely, when a shoal of kob does start feeding, the lines can be shortened to bring the shoal closer to the surface; when they're in a feeding frenzy they may even be caught on the surface.

When fishing for kob from a boat in deep waters, the depth of the water and the strength of the current dictate the type of tackle that will be needed. Fishermen operating along the east coast at places such as Port Alfred and East London, and along the KwaZulu-Natal coast, often use sinkers with a mass of up to 1 kilogram, as well as more sturdy tackle and even short boat rods with the ever-popular Scarborough reels. Because these rigs are fished to a depth of 100 metres or more, a number of hook traces baited with squid or fish are used.

Using live bait in a river produces excellent results, while a spinner slowly retrieved over a sandy bottom also does the trick.

When the sea is calm and the wind not too strong or blowing offshore, a ball or barrel sinker rig should be used in preference to a conventional sliding sinker rig, which prevents the live bait from swimming freely in the hole. A karanteen would serve the same purpose when live-bait fishing from the rocks.

THE HOOK-UP

Live- or drift-bait fishing produces exciting 'takes'. The live bait normally signals when a kob is about to grab it by its frantic swimming, which can be felt on the line. Once the kob has taken the bait, it moves off at a steady pace, often parallel to the shore. At this stage it is important to keep the reel in free-spool and allow sufficient time for the bait to be swallowed before setting the hook. Experience will teach you how much time to allow, but the novice can start off by counting slowly to 10 before setting the hook.

Remember that the hook must be sharp, and do not strike vigorously as you may snap the line. Merely lift the rod tip and let your drag setting do the rest and provided your line is in good condition you stand an excellent chance of landing it even with light or ultra-light tackle. Your drag should be set at a third of the breaking strain of your line, so for line of 6 kilograms you should set the drag at 2 kilograms. This can be done at home by attaching the line to a good quality spring scale and adjusting the drag until the line begins to peel off at a pull of 2 kilograms.

In comparison with most other species, kob are not classed as good fighting fish. However, specimens as large as 73 kilograms have been landed, and the sheer size of the fish can thoroughly test an angler's ability.

EATING QUALITY

Kob makes excellent eating and, particularly in the southwestern Cape, it is a sought-after table fish. Along the east coast the flesh is often infested with worms, especially those kob caught in the warmer waters of estuaries, but the worms are apparently harmless to man provided the flesh is properly cooked.

SHAD
(Pomatomus saltatrix)

Other common name: elf.

DISTRIBUTION

Shad, as it is known in KwaZulu-Natal and parts of the eastern Cape, is a powerful surface feeder that occurs along the entire South African coast. It is a highly migratory species, with the juveniles shoaling in the southwestern Cape and the adults migrating en masse to KwaZulu-Natal to spawn. Fishing mortality in the KwaZulu-Natal runs can approach 50 per cent but this is a fast-growing species and catch limits have resulted in a remarkable stock recovery. Shad also occurs in Australia and along parts of the American coast.

FEEDING HABITS

Shad are mostly found on sandy bottoms in reasonably clear water where there is a small beach break to provide the foamy water in which they like to feed. They are also found close to reefs and rocky outcrops – again, where there is foamy water.

They feed actively at dawn and dusk and are rarely caught in large numbers at night. They will also feed during the day, normally just before and on the high tide, when the sea is a ginger beer colour and wind swells continuously roll to the shore.

Shad feed on small fish such as karanteen and strepie beyond the breakers in calmer waters; they also feed on pelagic species such as anchovy and sardine (pilchard).

BAIT

Spinning is the more usual way of catching shad when they are feeding and is the favoured method used by shore anglers, but a cut-bait is usually used when they are not in a feeding mood and is the best way of locating them. Whole or cut sardines are ideal as are any other of the small bait species. Karanteen is a particularly good bait for shad – used either live or as a cut-bait.

WHERE TO CATCH

This species prefers warmer water and commonly occurs in sandy bays or shallow beaches from False Bay to Richards Bay and beyond. Along the west coast it enters lagoons and large river mouths where the temperature of the water may also be suitable. Small (mainly under-sized) shad are often caught in the mouth of the Berg River near Velddrif, while light-tackle enthusiasts have made good catches of shad weighing up to

8 kilograms, and even bigger in the warmer, top end of Langebaan Lagoon near Saldanha Bay.

In False Bay shad may appear as early as October, depending on when the southeasterly winds start to blow, but the shad fishing season only opens in December. Shad fishing in False Bay is good until April or May, or until the southeasters stop blowing.

During February and March ski-boat anglers fishing in False Bay, between Seal Island and the Strand, may encounter large shoals of shad feeding on the surface, whose presence is often given away by sea birds hovering over a shoal and darting down to pick up bits and pieces of baitfish kept on the surface by the feeding frenzy of the shad.

Along the east coast shad fishing is best in the winter months when the shoals migrate to KwaZulu-Natal to spawn. The shad larvae are then transported to the Cape coast by the Agulhas current which flows down the east coast of South Africa.

TACKLE AND TACTICS

Fishing from a boat Shad feeding on the surface can be caught by trolling small spinners (spoons) behind the boat and pulling them through the feeding shoal.

The choice of tackle to use when fishing for shad depends on the

The presence of predatory species is often given away by the frenzied activities of feeding sea birds.

location from which you choose to fish. Shad are generally in the 1-kilogram class (or lighter), particularly in KwaZulu-Natal, and as such, heavy tackle is normally not required. However, when fishing from a gently sloping beach, a longer cast and hence a longer rod – such as the standard 4- or 4,5-kilogram beach rod – is a very definite advantage. When fishing in protected bays and estuaries, or from a boat, the lighter the tackle the more fun you will have. A fixed spool-reel filled with 8-kilogram line will provide hours of enjoyment when fished with a light rod and a small sinker, or even when no sinker is used to cast the bait.

Fishing from the beach The standard rig for shad fishing from the beach is a grab sinker on either a sliding or a fixed rig and a long shank hook that may vary in size from 3/0 to 6/0. Always remember to use a short (approximately 10-centimetre) light steel trace on your hook (I use a 10-kilogram nylon-covered steel trace), as shad quite often bite off the hook, especially on an 'in bite', if you fish without a steel trace. Shad feed away from the bottom, so you must use a float on your hook trace to lift the bait away from the sea bed.

Fishing from the rocks Some Port Elizabeth shad fishermen use a special bait rig when fishing from the rocks into the foamy water of small bays. The night before, they prepare their bait by rigging a dozen or more whole sardines each on a thin steel trace with a clip-on swivel. The prepared bait is kept frozen and taken to the water in a coolbag. These anglers use fixed-spool reels (coffee grinders) on approximately 3-metre, quick-tapering rods. Because they stand on the rocks at the mouth of the bay they don't have to use a sinker to cast the bait. They clip on the bait trace and cast it on the edge of the foamy blue water close to the reef so that the bait just drifts. When the shad, normally weighing about a kilogram, grabs the bait the ensuing fight is an exciting experience. Once the shad has been landed the trace is unclipped, without removing the fish from the hook, and a fresh bait is clipped on. This enables the angler to present as many baits as possible during the time that the shoal is feeding.

Drift baits can also be used while fishing from a boat close inshore or in a bay. It is a good idea to have a drift bait on a small rod which you can leave in a rod holder. This serves as a 'trap line' while you fish on the bottom with a completely different set of tackle.

Spinning from boat and shore
Most anglers maintain that the most exciting way to catch shad – or, indeed, any predatory species – is by casting a spinner at the fish on the surface. A small spinner is used for shad, so make sure that you always have at least two in your tackle box. You never know when you will need them.

It is advisable to attach a short length of steel trace wire to your spinner, as feeding shad very easily chop off a spinner when they are biting fast and furiously.

Remember, when spinning for shad, the retrieval rate should be fairly slow. Modern reels have retrieval rates as high as 5,5:1 and 6:1, and an excited angler rapidly cranking away at such a reel may find he is either pulling the spinner so fast that the shad has difficulty taking it or, more important, that the fast retrieval rate has spoilt the action of the spinner, causing it to jump clear of the water and out of reach of the feeding shad.

Finding the ideal or most natural action of a spinner comes only with experience. By retrieving the spinner at different rates one soon notices when the action of the spinner through the water best resembles that of a frightened baitfish.

THE HOOK-UP
The manner in which shad take the bait may vary from day to day. They often tug at the bait and then swim away, pulling the rod tip down. On other occasions they may merely nibble at the bait, and you have to judge when to strike. They are also

fond of grabbing the bait and then swimming towards you. When this happens the shore angler's natural reaction is to run backwards, wind in the line and strike all at the same time. This can be a highly comical sight, especially when the angler manages to trip over his own tackle box. Instead of running backwards, the experienced angler slowly retrieves the slack line and waits for the fish to turn away before setting the hook.

The smaller shad that are most commonly caught are not strong fighters and are easily landed. The shad is, however, likely to jump out of the water when brought through the surf and may throw the hook or tear loose, especially if it is being pulled too hard.

EATING QUALITY
The flesh of fresh shad is excellent to eat but not after freezing so only keep what you can eat fresh.

WHITE MUSSELCRACKER
(Sparodon durbanensis)

Other common names: silver steenbras, brusher, white biskop, stompkop.

DISTRIBUTION
The white musselcracker occurs from Cape Point to just beyond Durban.

In the southern Cape the best catches are made during spring and summer, with October and November normally being the most productive. From East London to KwaZulu-Natal the spring months are best.

FEEDING HABITS

Like galjoen, white musselcracker feed in strong water that scours the gullies and exposes the various bait types that live in the sand – crabs, redbait and Venus ears (siffies) are their favourites.

BAIT

If you cannot obtain crab, redbait or Venus ears to use as bait, whole black mussels or white mussels (with or without the shell) are also attractive to musselcracker, while prawns, rock lobster and periwinkles can be used if all else fails.

WHERE TO CATCH

These fish occur in shoals but are also found in ones and twos, especially when they are big or feeding in the shallows. They are normally targeted in the deeper, churned-up water where they are found close to reefs on a sandy bottom but, like the galjoen, they are also caught in shallow, foamy water close to the shore. Because of their preference for these locations they are seldom caught from a boat.

If the water is calm and clear it is still possible to catch musselcracker, provided you are willing to get up early and you fish in a deep-water spot. In fact, these spots are sometimes only accessible when the sea is calm. A word of warning, though:

such localities can be extremely dangerous and it is best to fish them in the company of a local angler who knows the conditions well. Early morning or late afternoon is the best time of day to fish for this species.

TACKLE AND TACTICS

Along the Cape south coast white musselcracker is often found in places that are difficult to fish – that is, due to the rough water, the angler has to fish some distance above a gully or hole, and where it is not easy to land a fish. A sturdy set of tackle is essential to prevent the fish from cutting you off in the reefs.

The ideal tackle to fish with in this situation would be a 3- to 3,5-metre rod and a sturdy reel that has an anodised aluminium or steel spool which is not likely to burst under the strain. The reel should be filled with 17- or 20-kilogram breaking-strain nylon.

A thick line is an advantage when you are out to catch this fish, as it is a safeguard against being severed on rocks or reefs. A reel with a good drag system (large drag-washers) is also an advantage, because it enables you to put pressure on the fish and keep it away from the reefs or rocks.

Because of the white musselcracker's preference for rocky areas, it is advisable to use a strong, nylon hook trace (24-kilogram breaking strain or heavier) and a thin 12- or 15-kilogram sinker trace. A running sinker trace is best, especially when using crab as bait, as a musselcracker often bites shyly. With a running sinker trace it can pick up the bait without feeling the resistance of the sinker. The size of the sinker depends on the state of the sea and the class of the tackle you are using.

Use only the best quality hooks as this fish easily crushes and bends hooks with its powerful jaws. When fishing with crab as bait, an 8/0 is recommended because you can position the crab in the bight of the hook without having to push the hook through the carapace. The crab can be attached to the hook with elasticized cotton.

THE HOOK–UP

White musselcracker may take the bait and swim away rapidly, heading for the open sea or the closest rocks or reef. Or, if it happens to take the bait while swimming towards you, the line will go slack and you will have to wind it rapidly to feel the fish and set the hook. As with most species, there is no need to strike violently. By simply lifting the rod tip you will set the hook, provided your drag setting is correct and the hook is sharp.

EATING QUALITY

The flesh of a white musselcracker weighing up to 5 kilograms is deemed very good eating but the flesh of larger fish is coarse. The head makes an excellent soup.

Musselcracker is often caught from ledges that are dangerous to fish from, so be sure to keep an eye on the waves at all times.

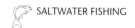

WHITE STEENBRAS
(Lithognathus lithognathus)

Other common name: pignose grunter.

DISTRIBUTION

This fish with its pig-like snout (source of its southern-Cape common, but not officially recognized, name of *varkbek*) is a popular sport-fish, as it gives such a good fight. It is found from the Orange River mouth in the Northern Cape to just south of Durban in KwaZulu-Natal. On the west coast it is often confused with *Lithognathus aureti* (west coast steenbras), which is found from St Helena Bay northwards along the coast of Namibia. When the two species are placed side by side it can be seen that the white steenbras has a more slender body than its west coast cousin and a sharper snout.

The white steenbras is a highly migratory species, with the adults migrating to eastern Cape waters to spawn, contrary to the popular misconception that they spawn in sandy bays, such as False Bay. Juveniles are fairly dependent on estuaries for their early growth and it appears that current stock declines can be at least partly attributed to estuarine degradation.

FEEDING HABITS

White steenbras have large fleshy lips and powerful gill covers which they use literally to blow food such as prawns, small crabs and worms out of the sand. Their favourite hunting grounds are the holes and sand-banks of shallow sandy beaches or in estuaries, where they are sometimes seen head down – their tails out of the water, thrashing the air – feeding on prawn banks. They may also be caught in rocky areas among redbait reefs.

BAIT
The favourite baits of this species are prawns, shrimps, small crabs, bloodworms and mussels. A sardine (pilchard), whole or cut up, or even a strip of squid (chokka) may also produce good results, especially when fishing for bigger specimens.

WHERE TO CATCH
Although it is classed as a summer fish, in False Bay and along the southwestern Cape coast white steenbras occurs throughout the year. Nonetheless, the best catches are made at the beginning and end of summer when some larger-sized specimens may be caught. Spring and early summer – the peak beach-seining or trek-netting period in False Bay – see big hauls of large white steenbras being made off the sandy beaches at Simon's Town, Strandfontein and Macassar. However, very few large specimens are caught by surf anglers, as these fish tend to feed on offshore prawn banks, beyond the normal casting range. The occasional large specimen may be taken during September, October and November, but usually under cover of darkness.

Elsewhere, good catches are made in or close to the mouths of large tidal rivers along the southern and eastern Cape coasts: the sandy stretches of beach at places such as Struisbaai, Kanon (near Mossel Bay), Keurboomsstrand (near Plettenberg Bay) and between the Gamtoos and Maitland rivers. Eastern Cape beaches are also favoured by surf anglers targeting this species.

TACKLE AND TACTICS
If you should hook one of the bigger specimens – 5 kilograms or larger – the fight of the white steenbras is something worth waiting for. They are known to take up to 50 metres of line on the initial run and, depending on the size of the fish and the breaking strain of the line, even to strip a reel. As a result, there are varying theories on the breaking strain of the line that should be used when fishing for this species. Most experienced anglers agree that the line used should be as light as possible and recommend the use of 8- or 10-kilogram breaking-strain line.

Surf fishing A grab or sand sinker may be required if the sea is rough and your bait is continuously being washed towards the shore. If the sea is calm it is best to use a conventional flat or bottle-shaped sinker

which will allow the bait to move around, increasing the chances of a white steenbras coming across it. It is best to use a sliding sinker rig as this will help to convince the fish that nothing will hinder his dash with the bait. Hook sizes depend on the size of the bait. Normally 3/0 to 6/0 hooks can be used with confidence. Some anglers prefer to use an additional hook which slides freely on the hook trace and is also hooked into the bait to make it look neat and attractive. Needless to say, this also improves the chances of hooking this fish.

Lagoon and estuary The calmer water of a lagoon or estuary will allow you to do battle with the white steenbras on light tackle. A light graphite rod of 2 to 2,5 metres in length and a fixed-spool reel filled with 6- or even 4-kilogram line will

Prawn beds in estuaries and lagoons are favourite feeding spots for white steenbras.

provide excellent sport, while fishing in calm water provides you with the best opportunity to present an enticing bait that may trap the unsuspecting white steenbras. A small ball sinker above the swivel of the hook trace and a 2/0 hook hidden in a prawn may be far more tempting to this fish than a sardine bait or bloodworm on a conventional rig. If conditions are absolutely ideal, with no wind or tidal current, it may even be possible to fish a prawn or a bloodworm without a sinker. This type of rig produces the most exciting takes anyone could wish for.

THE HOOK-UP

White steenbras have quite a reputation with anglers, and you need to be extra alert when trying to catch this species. It is renowned for its ability to remove the bait from a hook without the angler being aware of it and also, on the other hand, for grabbing the bait so violently that the rod can be pulled out of the hands of the unsuspecting angler.

Some anglers are convinced that when white steenbras come across a sinker, instead of taking the bait they take off with the sinker, while other anglers are of the opinion that they take the 'bung' on the hook trace. These diverse theories have been developed to try and explain the uncanny knack of the white steenbras of picking up the bait and taking off at a tremendous pace and then, despite the angler allowing plenty of time for the hook to be set, his not being able to hook the fish. This can make fishing for white steenbras a frustrating experience, as the fact that the fish has taken off like a steam train does not necessarily mean that you will hook or land it.

Once you have hooked a white steenbras, however, you are in for a fighting experience, particularly if you are fishing from the beach. A tenacious fighter, it never gives up and even once you have subdued it you still have to be careful when the fish enters the backwash at the edge of the beach. Do not attempt to pull the fish against the wash and never allow a helpful angler to lift the fish out of the water by grabbing your line. Your rod tip cushions the tension on the line while a direct pull can tear the hook out or even break the line. Be patient. Use the waves to bring your catch inshore and use the wave that washes up the beach to guide the fish out of the water.

EATING QUALITY

The creamy-white flesh of the white steenbras is excellent to eat grilled or pan-fried, as it has a fairly fine texture and a delicate flavour. It also makes a tasty pickled fish.

SHARKS AND RAYS

Sharks occur along the entire South African coastline and, although once regarded as a nuisance, they are now regarded as a prime sportfish.

The feats of the early boat and surf anglers who fished from Durban to Hermanus, the kite anglers of the former Transkei and eastern Cape, and the great white shark anglers of False Bay are well documented. Indeed, the last-mentioned exploited to the point of near extinction the False Bay population of great white sharks, which today are recognized for the important role they play as top predators. (For instance, they are the main predators of seals.)

Apart from the publicity the landing of a great white used to receive, the jaw, or even individual teeth, were sought after as collectors' items and fetched good prices. Today fishing for the great white shark is prohibited by law.

As far as present-day sportfishing is concerned, shark fishing has taken the pressure off the edible rock, surf and nearshore species. In addition, instead of bringing sharks to the weigh-in at the end of a day's fishing, tag-and-release angling competitions are used to test the skill and ability of competitive anglers without harming the population size of these cartilaginous fish, which produce very few young each year. (With the possible exception of tuna – when caught by rock and surf gamefishermen – sharks provide the greatest challenge to the angler, as they are the largest of the fish caught from the shore.)

Although many species of sharks are edible not many anglers take sharkmeat home for the table. In actual fact the flesh is quite tasty but it is necessary to clean shark as soon as it is landed. To do this, remove the head and tail and cut out the stomach and intestines. Leave the carcass to bleed in a rock pool for about 20 minutes, then skin and fillet it. Keep the fillets cool in clean sea water as this prevents an ammonia odour from developing, which happens if a shark is left in the sun. When fresh and fried in butter, it is difficult to distinguish sharkmeat from kingklip.

If you fish for sharks for the pure pleasure of hooking and landing a strong fighting fish, be sure to release your catch without harming it. By releasing it you will play an important role in protecting sharks from over-exploitation. (For tag-and-release details see page 229.)

SHARK FISHING TACKLE

The tackle required to do battle with these larger fighting fish does not differ to any great extent from the tackle that is normally used from the beach. A 4- to 4,5-metre beach rod with a heavy tip to cast the larger baits, and a reel with a line capacity of 250 to 300 metres is perfectly adequate. When fishing from the rocks the rod should be shorter (3,5 metres) but sturdy enough to control a large fish.

The terminal rig (hook and sinker trace) you choose depends on the breaking strain of the main line. If you are fishing for sharks with light line (of 10- or 12-kilogram breaking strain) on a beach rod, the line can very easily break when you put power into casting a heavy bait and sinker. By using a leader (a length of line of a heavier breaking strain, which can take the tension of the cast) a large bait can be cast without the main line breaking. The length of the leader will depend on the length of the rod, as a number of 'turns' should still be on the reel when the cast is made. The hook and sinker traces (nearly always a sliding sinker trace) are attached to the leader, and the thicker diameter of the leader provides added protection against the abrasive skin of the sharks, which may wear through a thin main line.

When you fish for 'toothy' species such as sharks you have to use a steel-wire trace. There are many factors that influence the diameter or breaking strain of the wire trace, and one of these factors is how ambitious you feel, how big a bait you wish to fish with and how far you have to cast it. A long steel-wire trace can be extremely cumbersome to cast and is normally easier to use when fishing from a boat than casting from a rocky headland or the beach.

Boat fishermen have another advantage over shore anglers in that they can swim a live bait such as a small shark, a shad or even a small kob. The smaller live baits are normally kept at the required depth by using a float or topbung but on the larger shark baits a balloon is used, tied to the main line. The balloon usually bursts as soon as the shark takes off and therefore is not a hindrance. This form of fishing provides much excitement because the live bait often swims to the surface, where you can watch it being taken.

Live baits are also relatively simple to swim from rocks or headlands where the water is deep. Some anglers swim a live bait through the surf by wading out as far as possible before casting or by letting it swim out in a rip current.

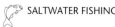

A spotted gully shark being tagged during a provincial angling competition at Struisbaai.

You need to use a large hook for shark fishing (a 10/0 or even a 12/0) as the baits you use are normally big. Make sure that the tip of the hook is not hidden by the bait and that it is as sharp as possible.

Remember to check your knots as you may have to wait quite a while for a bite, and to hook a large fish only to lose it as a result of poor tackle preparation is, to say the least, most frustrating.

Whether you fish from a boat or from the shore, creating a chum slick is certain to improve your chances of hooking a fish. Obviously fishing conditions must be suitable, with the wind not too strong and the sea being calm enough to establish a well-defined slick. The oily slick is caused by the natural oil in the pieces of fish used as chum, and by adding fresh pieces every now and then the chum slick will attract and hold an entire shoal and often put them into a feeding frenzy.

Creating such a slick is far easier from a boat than from the shore, but by continuously feeding small pieces of oily fish such as sardines into the water, the shore angler can achieve equally exciting results.

BROWN STINGRAY *(Dasyatis jenkinsii)*

Other common name:
sharpnose ray.

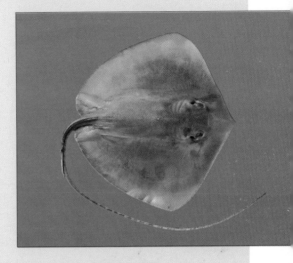

This ray occurs from East London to KwaZulu-Natal and beyond, where it is found in the shallow waters of the surf zone, in muddy estuaries and close to river mouths. The brown stringray does not grow as large as some of the other rays but makes up for its lack of bulk by being a strong fighter. It can be caught throughout the year but the best catches are made in December and January.

BLUE STINGRAY *(Dasyatis pastinaca)*

The blue stingray occurs along the entire coast of southern Africa and is the smallest and most commonly hooked ray. In the Cape it is hooked off sandy beaches during summer, often while the angler is fishing for kob. The best catches in KwaZulu-Natal waters are usually made between July and October. Although the diet of this species consists mainly of bottom-dwelling fish and organisms, the best bait to use is sardine (pilchard).

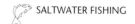

DIAMONDRAY *(Gymnura natalensis)*

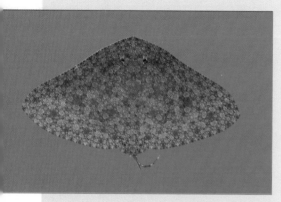

Other common names: butterflyray or backwater butterflyray.

This ray is one of the largest caught by anglers and, although not a strong fighter, is difficult to land. It is found from the eastern Cape to KwaZulu-Natal, where it is caught from sandy beaches or offshore banks. Large specimens are caught in summer north of the Tugela River, while in winter diamondrays follow the sardine shoals and are caught on sardine and even on lures.

HONEYCOMB STINGRAY *(Himantura uamak)*

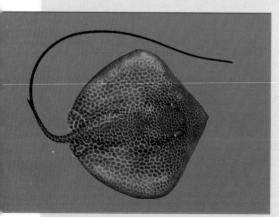

Other common names: marbled or leopard stingray.

The honeycomb ray is the largest of the rays and has a reputation of being a very strong fighter and difficult to land. It is caught in estuaries and off shallow bays from the southern Cape to the Mozambican border and beyond. It has a small mouth and is normally caught on small baits such as sardine and mackerel.

This ray is caught in summer and can thoroughly test the angler's ability and strength It can fight for hours – and normally win the battle. An angler who lands a honeycomb ray will find himself exhausted and very stiff and sore the next day. Both this ray and most other rays can cause a serious injury with its tail whose errated spines near the base can cause very bad and painful cuts.

BLACKTIP SHARK *(Carcharhinus limbatus)*

Other common name: blackfin shark.

This strong, agile shark occurs in mid-water close to the shore from Knysna to KwaZulu-Natal and beyond. Although not as common as they once were, they are caught on the north coast during the summer months, when they come close to the shore to feed on mullet. They are very exciting to catch as they take off at great speed on the first run, sometimes leaping clear of the water. They can be caught on a live or dead bait and are good eating.

COPPER SHARK *(Carcharhinus brachyurus)*

Other common names: bronze whaler, narrow-tooth shark.

Copper sharks are caught along the entire west coast and as far as Durban on the east coast. They prefer cooler waters and are very plentiful from False Bay to Mossel Bay.

Also known as 'bronzies', copper sharks swim close to the bottom, where they feed on slow-swimming fish like small sharks, skates, sole and squid. Any fish bait or a strip of squid is suitable as bait. (A piece of polystyrene foam inserted into your fish bait will keep it off the bottom, away from crabs.)

Good catches of this species are also made off the eastern Cape coast and the south coast of KwaZulu-Natal, especially during the winter sardine run.

DUSKY SHARK
(Carcharhinus obscurus)

Other common name: ridgeback grey shark.

The dusky shark is found from Cape Agulhas to the north coast of KwaZulu-Natal and is probably the most common shark in KwaZulu-Natal waters. It can grow as large as 400 kilograms, but the bigger specimens are not caught from the shore as they prefer the deeper offshore waters.

In KwaZulu-Natal the population of small dusky sharks occurring near the beach has grown to a considerable size. More than likely this is the result of the large sharks that are their natural predators having been removed from the food chain by the anti-shark nets in place along all the popular bathing beaches.

Young dusky sharks feed close to the shore and are often caught on fish baits such as mackerel, shad, sardine and mullet. They are capable of biting through nylon trace, so a short wire trace is necessary when fishing for this species.

The flesh of the dusky shark is good to eat but, as in the case of most shark flesh, it must be filleted and skinned soon after the fish has been caught. (See page 126.)

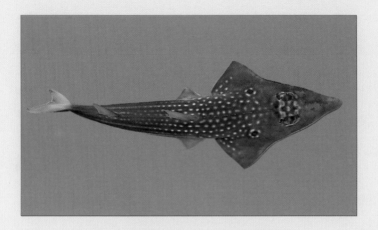

GIANT GUITARFISH
(Rhynchobatus djeddensis)

Other common name: giant sandshark

Many species of guitarfish are caught off the beaches around the southern African coastline, but two in particular are of interest to the angler: the lesser and the giant guitarfish. The lesser guitarfish occurs from Saldanha Bay to KwaZulu-Natal and beyond, and in the Cape many a young angler has 'earned his spurs' by catching a guitarfish shark from the beach while dad was busy fishing for kob or shad. The guitarfish takes the bait – normally a fish bait such as sardine – with vigour and puts up a surprisingly good fight for its size.

The giant guitarfish, or 'sandy', is one of the most popular angling fishes of KwaZulu-Natal, where it is known as a strong fighter. It varies in size between 25 and 86 kilograms, with some larger than 100 kilograms being hooked each year – but only a few landed. It is caught from the beach in shallow, discoloured water and prefers big bait such as mackerel or shad heads but will also take fish bait cutlets or fillets, or other bait such as rock lobster and squid.

The flesh of guitarfish is considered to be good eating but few people are acquainted with it. Perhaps this is just as well, though, as it is good policy to return these fish to the sea to fight another day.

SOUPFIN SHARK *(Galeorhinus galeus)*

Other common name: vaalhaai.

The soupfin shark is very common in Cape waters and until the introduction of a synthetic vitamin A, it supported a commercial fishery for its liver oil. These days it is caught mainly for its flesh. Along the southern Cape coast the best catches are made during the winter months but as these sharks hardly ever grow bigger than 30 kilograms, they do not offer much of a challenge to the angler.

Soupfin sharks are caught mostly by boat anglers, as they feed in deeper water close to the bottom on bottom-living species such as hake and gurnard. Soupfin sharks take fish bait such as sardine (pilchard) and squid (chokka) and, as they feed in shoals, large catches are always likely.

Anglers visiting Hermanus should make the effort to drive through to Gans-baai harbour, where commercial soupfin shark catches are landed and processed, and take the opportunity to sample some *vaalhaai* biltong, which can be purchased at the fishermen's co-op in the harbour.

SPOTTED GULLY SHARK *(Triakis megalopterus)*

Other common name: sweet william.

Of all the strong fighting sharks the spotted gully shark and the hound shark are probably the two most commonly caught. Although they are found along the entire west coast and as far east as East London, they are very popular in the southwestern and southern Cape, where they sometimes can be seen feeding next to rocky outcrops on beaches in or near the surf zone. On occasion they all but beach themselves in chasing their prey into the beach break.

These sharks will take most of the baits they happen to come across, though their natural diet is small fish, crabs and other small crustaceans. They often take the bait of the unsuspecting panfish angler who, using light tackle, is not expecting such a large fish. The fight is normally quick and one-sided, as the spotted gully shark will swim for the nearest rock or reef, where the trace or main line becomes snagged and breaks.

The best time to fish for spotted gully and hound sharks is during the summer months, particularly from December to February. In False Bay these sharks sometimes cause great excitement among the shark-fishing fraternity when they congregate in shoals, providing excellent sportfishing, especially for those fishermen who are prepared to take them on with light tackle.

CHAPTER SEVEN

ESTUARINE AND INSHORE BOAT FISHING

A panoramic view of Knysna Lagoon, showing some of the characteristic features of estuaries and lagoons: mud flats, sandbanks and channels. As nurseries and feeding grounds for many of the popular angling species, every effort should be made to conserve such areas in an undeveloped, undamaged and unsilted state.

The light-tackle boat enthusiasts who prefer to fish in the calmer waters of tidal rivers, lagoons, harbours and bays are very fortunate in that many such localities can be found at relatively short intervals along the entire southern African coast, especially along the southern and eastern seaboards.

KWAZULU-NATAL

In KwaZulu-Natal, apart from the numerous smaller lagoons and river mouths, St Lucia, the Umfolozi River, Richards Bay, the Mlalazi River (near Mtunzini) and Durban harbour, are some of the more popular spots, yielding Natal stumpnose, spotted grunter, kob, garrick and occasionally giant kingfish.

CAPE

In the area of the eastern Cape that was formerly known as the Transkei, the picturesque estuarine resorts are firm favourites among keen anglers. They have become renowned for the excellent sport they are known to offer, particularly the catching of angling favourites, such as white steenbras, spotted grunter and kob. The true enthusiast who has a four-wheel-drive vehicle and uses a car-top dinghy can also fish most of the lesser known rivers and lagoons situated along the coast, often with most noteworthy results. Port St Johns and Qora Mouth are two of the better-known small-boat fishing regions.

Further south along the coast, Kei Mouth is a very popular fishing site, while the Keiskamma and Great Fish rivers are favoured by those visiting the former Ciskei region. Both of these rivers are particularly well known for producing a number of excellent kob catches.

Estuarine anglers who direct their attention to the eastern Cape have the particularly good fortune of being able to choose from numerous tidal rivers, such as the Kowie, Kariega, Bushmans, Sundays, Swartkops and Gamtoos. All of these rivers are famous for the bags of kob, garrick, shad, spotted grunter and white steenbras that they produce.

In the southern Cape small-boat fishing in rivers and lagoons such as the Keurbooms River, Knysna Lagoon and the Gouritz, Kafferkuils and Breede rivers offers good catches of kob, spotted grunter, white steenbras and garrick.

Closer to Cape Town, the Hermanus and Bot river lagoons are popular small-boat angling spots, where kob, garrick, white steenbras and shad are caught, while in Langebaan Lagoon near Saldanha Bay on the west coast various species of sharks, large shad, kob and good catches of white stumpnose can be made, usually during the summer months.

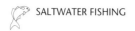

ESTUARINE FISHING

Although there are many species that can be caught in tidal rivers and lagoons, the fishing is seasonal (mainly spring and summer) and the fish are usually more difficult to catch than those in the sea, though by using light tackle, good bait and different techniques good catches are not impossible.

Fishing in estuaries is tide-dependent. The tide affects both bait-collecting and the feeding patterns of the target fish. The incoming tide is generally the best tide on which to fish, especially on the tidal flats, where bait can be collected during low tide. Although the water may be very shallow over the prawn banks, white steenbras and spotted grunter often move in to feed on the worms, small prawns and crabs that have been dislodged or disturbed while the angler collected his bait.

When fishing in an unfamiliar tidal river, use the spring low tide to look for the best places to fish. Deep holes are good spots for kob, while the slopes of the prawn flats are good places to anchor or drift for bottom feeders such as white steenbras, spotted grunter and bream, or fish a live bait for garrick.

There is good fishing to be had in an estuary or bay by drifting instead of anchoring – as long as there is little or no wind and the current is not strong. Many species of bottom feeders, especially in bays, prefer certain localities and by drifting over what may appear to be a featureless rocky bottom you may come across some of the 'hot spots'.

The strength of the wind and the direction from which it is blowing also play a role in estuary or river fishing, as the boat is normally anchored, fore and aft, across the current to keep it from swinging around and to enable the spreading of the baits. This can be done only when the wind is not blowing too hard and the tidal current, especially outgoing, is not too strong. If you are uncertain about whether the conditions are safe, rather anchor the boat with the bow into the wind and fish with fewer rods.

SAFETY FIRST

Storage space is always a problem on a small boat. Tackle boxes, live-bait tanks or buckets, bait and sets of rods and reels take up a lot of space and there may be the temptation to leave some of the safety equipment behind if you feel you are fishing on 'safe' waters. Never take the chance. Large tidal rivers can become very rough when a strong wind blows against the current. The short, choppy wind swell that builds up can be very dangerous if you are fishing from a small, open dinghy. Should conditions become unsafe, head for the river bank, pull the boat clear of the water and walk back to base. If you are too far from your base, wait for the tide to turn, as conditions will become calmer when the tide and the wind are both moving in the same direction.

Always carry all the required safety equipment and make sure that everybody on board knows where it is stored. Small-boat owners often use odd nooks and crannies to store 'non-fishing' gear in order to leave room for fishing. Avoid storing safety equipment where it cannot be reached in a hurry.

A good anchor is an essential part of boating equipment. Grapnel-type anchors are very popular among small-boat anglers as they are light and easy to store, and grip equally well on muddy and rocky bottoms. Make sure that the anchor chain is long and heavy enough, as the correct combination of length and mass will stop the anchor from dragging.

BOAT DESIGN

The design and layout of the boat you buy – even a small, inshore ski-boat – will depend largely on intended launching sites. At places such as False Bay, Hermanus, Struisbaai, Mossel Bay, Knysna and Port Elizabeth the inshore boat anglers can launch their craft at recognized launching ramps that offer safe launching in varying wind and sea conditions. It is therefore possible to fit large windscreens or cabins to these boats as the launch does not entail going through the surf zone, and smaller outboards can also be used, making the boats more economical to run.

These boats differ markedly from the crafts launched from beaches along the KwaZulu-Natal coastline where, regardless of size, boats do not have cabins or large windscreens as they must be capable of punching through the shore-break. They are also usually fitted with two powerful outboard motors to ensure that, in the event of a motor breakdown, the boat can return safely to shore on one motor. All the fishing tackle as well as other equipment has to be stored in a hatch or tied down, as everything may be lost if the boat should turn over. A beach launch may also require the use of a four-by-four vehicle to get the rig near the water, adding yet another exciting item to the shopping list of the prospective boat angler.

An echosounder (fish finder) is a definite asset to have on board, regardless of the size of the boat or whether you choose to fish in an estuary or a bay. Finding the correct type of ground, or even locating shoals of fish, can be successfully done with very little guidance or experience. Echosounders are relatively inexpensive and will certainly help to improve your catches.

A tranquil setting at Kosi Bay – ideal terrain for the light-tackle boat angler.

CAPE SNOEK
(Thyrsites atun)

If ever there was a species that triggers the anything-that-floats fleet to put to sea, it is the Cape snoek. While it can hardly be described as a good fighting fish, landing and subduing a wriggling snoek without being bitten is a learned skill, and the pure excitement of catching this fish – which will grab any lure or bait when it is on the bite – becomes an addiction that is difficult to understand unless you have experienced it for yourself.

DISTRIBUTION
Historically, snoek made their appearance on the west coast of South Africa in the region of Port Nolloth and then migrated southwards around the Cape Peninsular as far east as Port Elizabeth. In recent times, due to the collapse of the Namibian sardine (pilchard) stock the snoek have moved to the southwestern Cape where they may often be caught year-round.

FEEDING HABITS
Snoek feed on pelagic shoal fish and are therefore found mostly in coastal waters. At certain times of the year, however, they move offshore to follow the shoals.

BAIT
Pelagic shoalfish such as sardines, redeye (Atlantic round herring) and anchovies make the best bait.

WHERE TO CATCH
On the west coast the best catches of snoek are made by line- and ski-boat anglers fishing between Lambert's Bay and Yzerfontein, and at Dassen

A successful morning's snoeking in False Bay.

Island. Nearer to Cape Town, snoek are caught near Robben Island and along the western side of the Cape Peninsula, while Hout Bay becomes the centre of activity when shoals appear on the eastern side of the Peninsula. Occasional catches are made along the southern Cape coast but they are rarely as successful as those made on the west coast.

Snoek are normally in peak condition during the winter months and it is during this time that they undertake their migration down the west coast to the Cape Peninsula. It is very likely that this migration is linked to that of the shoals of juvenile sardines and anchovies which are on their return journey from the west coast to the Agulhas Bank at this time.

False Bay boat anglers usually catch snoek late in the season – in July, August and September – but at this stage the fish are in very poor condition: thin and full of cestode parasites, which the fishermen refer to as worms or *melkare*. Although the 'worms' do not affect the quality of the flesh they certainly make it look less tempting. Snoek are also prone to a parasitic infection that makes the flesh go soft and powdery; these specimens are referred to as *papsnoek* by the fishermen.

Shore anglers fishing off ledges at places such as Rooikrans and Rooiels in False Bay occasionally catch snoek during August and September. During this time, snoek shoals move very close to the shore when the water is calm, within range of anglers spinning from ledges. A slow retrieval rate is vital, to allow the spinner to sink well below the surface where the passing shoals occur. Because they are in poor condition at this time they do not put up a fight and are not particularly rewarding to catch. As a result spinner fishermen usually release the snoek they catch from the shore.

TACKLE AND TACTICS
Fishing from a boat To catch snoek in any great quantities, and to avoid wasting time untangling lines, as you would if you used a rod and reel, you should use a handline. The pace of the fishing is such that all the lines normally go *vas* (a full-house strike) at the same time, and if you cannot

control the snoek on your line it is bound to cause the most unbelievable tangle.

Serious snoek fishermen also vary the thickness of their lines, depending on how the snoek are biting. When the snoek are shy and reluctant to take the bait they use thin lines, normally less than 40 kilograms in breaking strain, though sometimes as light as 20 kilograms. As soon as the shoal starts biting, the thin lines are rolled up and heavy-duty handlines of 60- or 70-kilogram breaking strain are used. This way the fishermen catch more snoek, and by pulling fast, they keep the lines clear of each other.

If you are fishing for the sheer pleasure of hooking and landing a snoek, and you don't mind the odd tangle or bite-off, then light tackle is the best to use. Snoek are not strong fighters and can be landed on 6- or even 4-kilogram line, but as they are members of the 'razor gang' a steel-wire or a thick nylon trace is essential.

Sardines are the most popular bait for this species and are used whole or as cutlets on a large hook such as a 10/0 or 11/0. A snoek dolly (or *bokstang*) consists of a chromed or painted cigar-shaped lead with a skirt and a barbless hook. It is the best lure to use when the snoek are on the bite and is fished on a 60- or 70-kilogram line. The thicker handline is easier to grip and pull, especially when you are using *vinger-lappies*. These are made from neoprene rubber or other similar material and are worn on the fore and small finger of each hand to prevent them being cut by the line.

Snoek fishermen either troll the dollies behind a slow-moving boat or throw the dolly away from the side of a stationary boat, allowing it to sink to a set depth before retrieving it with a jerky movement. Some days snoek take the dollies readily and may be boated at a furious pace.

THE HOOK-UP

When the snoek are not biting voraciously they tend to mouth the bait. In such cases, if you are fishing with a handline, a good ploy would be to allow the fish to move away steadily (taking about 1 metre of line) before striking against it. If you are fishing with a rod and reel, allow the rod to dip to a horizontal position and then set the hook by lifting the rod.

NOTE

* *Whether fishing from the shore or from a boat, be very careful when handling a hooked snoek. Apart from the sharpness of its teeth, some anglers believe that there is an anti-coagulating substance in the mucus on the teeth, as the bite of a Cape snoek takes a long time to stop bleeding. Experienced snoek fishermen maintain that the best way to stop the bleeding is to apply to the wound the liquid from the eye of a snoek!*

* *If you intend taking a snoek home to eat, fleck it during a lull in the fishing and salt it with coarse salt. If you do not have time on the boat, do so as soon as you come ashore. Leave the salt for at least an hour, then rinse it off. This will help to prevent the snoek from going 'pap'.*

EATING QUALITY

Snoek is one of the traditional South African table fish, and although very bony the flesh is exceptionally tasty. It is an ideal fish for braaiing but it is equally good fried, baked or smoked.

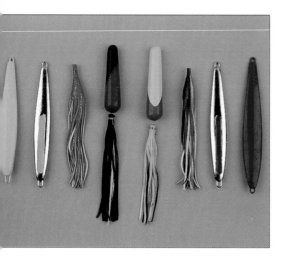

A selection of snoek lures.

'COUTA
(Scomberomorus commerson)

Other common names: king mackerel, *katonkel.*

Also known as 'dart', but not offi-cially recognized as such, the 'couta is one of the east coast's prime angling species. It is commonly found along the east coast, but has been taken as far south as Mossel Bay. The main part of the 'couta stock resides off Mozambique, and KwaZulu-Natal catches are dependent on the seasonal migration of the species into local waters.

FEEDING HABITS
'Couta shoals normally feed over pinnacles, though the larger fish are fond of patrolling shallower water and are often caught a few hundred metres beyond the back-line. Its favoured baitfish types are mackerel,

mullet, boneys, shad, sardine, squid and small reef fish such as slinger and roman.

BAIT
All of the above species are ideal as live or dead bait.

WHERE TO CATCH
The best time to fish for 'couta is early morning or late afternoon. Blue oceanic water is where they are nor-mally found, though they are also located at 'weedlines', floating objects or at colour changes such as at the edge of brown river-water running into the sea

Along the KwaZulu-Natal coastline there is a summer and a winter season for 'couta. The summer season is from the end of November to March, when shoals of 'couta may be found from Cape Vidal to Shelly Beach. At this time of year 'couta are normally small (2 to 10 kilograms in weight) and swim in fairly large shoals.

The winter season normally starts in April and lasts until after the sardine run when bigger 'couta (some as large as 30 kilograms) are caught. The larger fish are commonly referred to as 'crocodiles' and are known to swim in pairs or small shoals. The larger they grow, however, the more likely you are to find single fish. Smaller 'couta, although not so abundant in winter, may still be caught, especially during the sardine run.

This fish has razor-sharp teeth and must be treated with respect, even when dead. This feature, together with its streamlined shape and ability to rapidly change direction, makes it lethal when it hits a shoal of baitfish.

TACKLE AND TACTICS

During the summer months, the average boat angler would use tackle ranging from 8 to 24 kilograms. The rods used for 'couta are longer than those used for tuna fishing as the fish tends to fight on the surface where a longer pull or 'stroke' is needed to coax it to the boat.

This species is an excellent light-tackle gamefish. In fact, the lighter you choose to fish the more likely you are to get strikes and the greater the pleasure of catching the fish will be. 'Couta can be taken by spinning (spooning) from a boat or by trolling with lines or bait, or drifting with live or dead bait.

Spinning or spooning This method of catching 'couta (from a drifting or anchored boat and using a long, V-back spoon) has been developed into something of an art in KwaZulu-Natal. The spoon is let down as close to the bottom as possible and then 'whipped' back to the boat. This 'whipping' creates the action of a darting baitfish and is achieved by lifting the rod up and down while the spoon is being retrieved. As the 'couta often strikes from the side, it is a good idea to attach a loose-swinging single hook to the pulling-point of the spoon.

Trolling The most common method of catching 'couta is by trolling, particularly when looking for shoals, and the most popular and successful lures are Rapalas, though ski-boat anglers also take along the more common feather and plastic lures. (Green mackerel, blue mackerel, red head and fluorescent orange are the most popular Rapalas used.) Generally green and silver, and red and white are the most common lure colours, though 'hot pink' seems to be the all-round favourite. Darker colours and reds are used early in the morning, while lighter colours such as the yellows are used at midday. As 'couta have very sharp teeth the lures must be rigged on wire traces (nos. 5 to 9 single-strand piano-wire traces are commonly used.) The ideal trolling speed is between 4 and 5 knots.

Bait fishing This is the most exciting and challenging form of 'couta fishing, for with its excellent eyesight a 'couta will readily take a well-rigged and -presented bait, while totally ignoring any shoddily prepared baits.

Here are a few rules to remember when fishing with dead or live baits:
* The bait must be in prime condition: as fresh as possible or, in the case of live baits, as frisky as possible.
* The bait must not spin when trolled. It can swim on its side or upside-down but it must not spin.
* Your hook should be carefully concealed, and the bait must appear as natural as possible.
* When rigging a dead or a live bait for trolling, the 'pulling point' must always be at the 'nose' of the fish, and hooks placed in the side of the body should not restrict the action of the bait. Baits can be made to swim deeper or straighter by attaching a Mydo head or a Bait-o-matic.
* Bait should be trolled about 8 to 12 metres behind the boat and the best trolling speed is achieved by using one motor just in gear.

Drift fishing is another popular way of catching this species, especially when it is feeding deeper or is shy to take a bait. This is done with live bait or with carefully rigged dead bait, but despite the care put into the preparation of live or dead

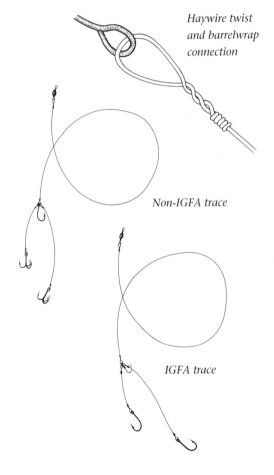

Haywire twist and barrelwrap connection

Non-IGFA trace

IGFA trace

The 'couta trace.

bait, the 'couta is also known to take strip or fillet bait intended for other species.

The rigging of live and dead bait depends on whether the angler plans to fish according to IGFA (International Game Fishing Association) tournament rules or whether he is fishing for the pot. Treble hooks, not permissible when fishing tournament rules, are more effective in hooking a fish, though single hooks are less likely to pull out.

Shore fishermen 'Couta can be caught from the beach or rocky headlands using conventional beach fishing tackle and by spooning, especially when the sardine shoals are around, or with live bait, such as shad, that are either swum out from the shore on a 'topbung' (surface float), or by casting the sinker out and clipping on the live bait and allowing it to swim down the line.

The common non-IGFA rig is prepared by using two or three no. 1 or 1/0 treble hooks in line on a single-strand piano-wire trace. One treble is hooked through the nose of the fish, while the second is embedded in the body. The last treble hook is placed near the tail.

The IGFA trace is made up with two no. 4 to 6/0 single hooks; one in each side of the body of the bait with a bent wire at the pulling point (through the nose of the fish).

THE HOOK-UP

'Couta are known to 'chop' the bait from the side and often will frustrate the angler by just nipping off the tail of the bait. Keep checking your bait, as you may never be aware that a 'couta is having a go at it. The hook-up, however, is immediate and there is no real need to 'strike' the fish as it tends to hook itself when running against the strike drag setting.

The initial run of a 'couta is normally long with the fish staying on or near the surface. After that it may take two or three further runs before being brought to the boat. A big fish will tend to stay 10 to 15 metres away from the boat, shaking its head with its mouth wide open. This is a critical stage of the fight, as the fish should be allowed to have its way without giving it slack line. A wrong move here will most certainly tear the hooks out.

At this stage a sinker or a weighted head (the Mydo head or the Bait-o-matic) may help the fish to throw the hook out of the mouth. By shaking his head, the 'couta may also cause the wire to kink or even snap. Once alongside, however, it is docile and can easily be tagged or gaffed.

EATING QUALITY

The tasty white flesh makes 'couta a fine table fish.

GIANT KINGFISH
(Caranx ignobilis)

DISTRIBUTION

The giant kingfish is the biggest and most powerful of the approximately 15 tropical kingfish that are caught along the coastline of southern Africa from the Kei River, beyond Mozambique and well into the central Indian Ocean. Although occasionally caught off East London, it seldom, if ever, occurs further south.

As its name implies, this species can attain a huge mass – 50 kilograms and larger, although the average size caught tends to be below 20 kilograms. For rock and surf anglers it is a truly memorable experience to do battle with this powerful fighter – a battle that will tax the strength of both the angler and his tackle.

FEEDING HABITS

The giant kingfish will eat almost anything that is available, including baby turtle. In the shallows it feeds on small fish such as pinky, blacktail, karanteen and shad; at the edge of reefs its main diet is mantis shrimp, squid (chokka) and various crustaceans. When in deeper water, it tends to feed on skipjack (bonito), slinger and other redfish.

A giant kingfish caught at St Lucia.

BAIT

Because this species is so attracted to a moving bait, live bait is the obvious choice for the angler wherever the terrain allows it. A frisky live bait such as skipjack, pinky, slinger, or shad (elf), is ideal, and it will also take a fillet bait; however, spoons and Rapalas are equally successful in catching this fish.

WHERE TO CATCH

Unlike most other gamefish, giant kingfish are within the reach of most anglers as they are equally at home in the shallows of the surf zone, off rocky points and ledges, in harbours and lagoons, and in deeper water. Prime catching spots in KwaZulu-Natal are Protea Reef and Aliwal Shoal, as well as the ledges of the north coast.

Giant kingfish can be caught during the day, though early morning and late afternoon are best. They are found all year round, but tend to be more active in autumn and winter when the baitfish are abundant.

TACKLE AND TACTICS

Anglers adept at using a Scarborough reel may well be able to cope successfully with the first furious run of the kingfish; the rest of us, however, are more at home with a multiplying reel capable of holding 250 to 300 metres of at least 16-kilogram breaking-strain nylon and with a good drag system. That, coupled with a sturdy rod similar to one used for yellowtail, will give you a good chance of bringing a giant kingfish to the gaff.

When fishing with a live bait, spoon or plug, the trace should be thick enough (about 37-kilogram breaking strain) to withstand the damage done to it by the powerful jaws of the giant kingfish. The scutes running along the lateral line on the near flanks of the fish are very sharp and may also damage the line, especially when the fish is moving away from the angler and the line runs close to its body. The length of the trace will depend on where you are fishing. From a boat you can use as long a trace as is necessary (up to 1,5 metres), but when fishing from the shore select a length that is going to be comfortable to cast.

The aggressive kingfish loves to take a spoon when the mood suits it. The spoon can be worked very effectively from either shore or boat, but the trick is to know where the fish is lurking near the drop-offs or ledges and then to work the spoon through the most likely area.

The live-bait rig recommended is the one used for most shore game-fish species with a treble or single hook placed either in front of or behind the dorsal fin.

If you are fishing from a ski-boat, a more powerful short rod such as a 15-kilogram stand-up stick, with a strong multiplying reel, would be the tackle to use for live- or dead-bait fishing. If you should favour casting a spoon or surface plug for giant kingfish, however, then the longer spinning rod, already described in chapter three, would be most suitable.

THE HOOK-UP

The giant kingfish is a powerful and fast swimmer and its initial run after taking a bait or line may be as long as 200 metres, if not more. Anglers using reels with insufficient line capacity, therefore, may suffer the indignity of being cleaned out! If you are fishing in deep water from a boat, the fish will take full advantage of the depth in which you hook it and will bore down with a stubborn and back-breaking action, usually making for the reef, where it will try to cut off the line.

After the initial run the fight consists of short bursts of power and it requires grim determination and concentration on the part of the angler to win back every inch of line. However, when the kingfish tires he is easily brought to the gaff.

As the fight can be a lengthy process, sometimes more than an hour, it is very important that your rod bucket should be strong and comfortable enough to provide the all-important support throughout the fight. It goes without saying that a strong and sharp gaff (and somebody who is experienced in handling it) is an essential part of the tackle, and venturing down to the water's edge without one would be extremely foolhardy.

EATING QUALITY

The flesh of the smaller giant kingfish (under 20 kilograms) is very tasty but should never be overcooked as it has a tendency to dryness.

QUEEN MACKEREL
(Scomberomorus plurilineatus)

Other common name: Natal snoek.

Less well known than many other species, the queen mackerel is the favourite of most anglers who do know it, as it is a cunning fish and difficult to catch. Though commonly referred to as 'snoek' by KwaZulu-Natal anglers, it is not related to the true Cape snoek.

DISTRIBUTION
Queen mackerel are found on the east coast of Africa, from the eastern Cape to Kenya. This is the only population in the world and, as with many other species, catches are declining.

FEEDING HABITS
The diet of the queen mackerel consists of smaller fish species, along with squid (chokka), crabs and swimming prawns, which they attack at high speed, their extremely sharp teeth chopping them to pieces.

BAIT
Any of the above are ideal as bait but strips of sardine (pilchard) or skipjack (bonito) are good for trolling.

WHERE TO CATCH
St Lucia attracts queen mackerel throughout the year, and further north the odd shoal can also be found year-round, but to the south this species is at its most plentiful during autumn and winter when the baitfish move into KwaZulu-Natal waters. Hot spots are river mouths, such as at Unkomaas, and headlands with shallow reefs. Queen

mackerel usually swim in shoals or pairs and are seldom found in water deeper than 10 metres.

TACKLE AND TACTICS

Rock and surf anglers have little joy with this species except when there is plenty of baitfish action and the queen mackerel start to feed in a frenzy, which might result in a hook-up. A live bait or a spoon is just about the only way to entice it into attacking. Tackle similar to that used for garrick or shad is ample as they fight in bursts of straight runs and tire easily. Always use a wire trace as these fish have razor-sharp teeth.

Ski-boaters use feathers and small Rapalas trolled at a speed of 6 knots to lure the queen mackerel if it is around. Again, a wire trace is essential (about no. 4 is perfect). Keep a spinning outfit handy, as once you hook up, the shoal tends to mill around and will readily accept a well-presented, shiny smaller spoon. Coffee grinder reels are ideal.

Trolling rigs again must be of light tackle, nothing more than 10 kilograms. Rods and reels should be similar to that of 'couta tackle (2- to 2,3-metre rods and fast-retrieve multiplying reels).

If you are slow-trolling for 'couta or bigger gamefish and you notice that queen mackerel are about, rig a strip of sardine or skipjack on a single hook, wrap it up with cotton and troll it behind a small plastic skirt out behind the bigger baits. You may well be lucky. If you are targeting queen mackerel and they go off the bite but you can still see them jumping and feeding, take a Mydo bait-swimmer and use it as a downplaner. Just tie the Mydo (no. 3 or 4) where the swivel would be and select a lure – a Clarke spoon or a Huntington drone are recommended. This Mydo trick eliminates the spinning associated with these lures and will almost always bring queen mackerel back on the bite.

THE HOOK-UP

Like the 'couta, the queen mackerel attacks at high speed, continuing the run as it feels the hook and pressure. It then turns back to the angler, and it is at this point that most catches are lost, as this fish has a very soft mouth and shakes its head from side to side fast and jerkily trying to shake out the hook. The trick is to pull hard while its head is towards you, but as it draws near it will run again at high speed, repeating the pattern before being landed. This fish is thin and slippery and a sharp gaff is required.

EATING QUALITY

The pure white juicy flesh of the queen mackerel is quite delicious and highly sought after.

RED STEENBRAS
(Petrus rupestris)

DISTRIBUTION

The red steenbras is found from False Bay to just beyond Durban.

Although once a popular shore-angling species, today it is seldom caught from the shore. In fact, the number of red steenbras in the inshore regions has been so drastically reduced that catching this fish in any quantity is the exception rather than the rule. The large spawning adults are commonly found off the eastern Cape coast and the adults in the offshore reefs of the Agulhas Bank, while the juveniles occur in the coastal waters of the south-western Cape.

FEEDING HABITS

The red steenbras is a predator and feeds on smaller fish such as the *blou steentjie, fransmadam* and small roman. Octopus too are part of their diet, while the smaller red steenbras are also partial to klipfish.

BAIT

In addition to the above species, red steenbras are attracted to oily baits, and a fillet of skipjack (bonito) or even Cape snoek can produce good results. When fishing on reefs where small fish are a nuisance, a *steentjie* or any small fish rigged as a live bait may work well.

WHERE TO CATCH

Despite the scarcity of this fish, regular catches continue to be made on the Agulhas Bank and along the eastern Cape coast but almost always only from boats. Generally speaking, the further off-shore and the deeper the reefs, and the more off-the-beaten-track the reefs are, the greater is the likelihood of making reasonable catches.

If you find a pinnacle on an echo-sounder, the best place to fish for this species is at the base of the pinnacle in deep water. Smaller fish tend to swim around the top of the pinnacle, but red steenbras go right to the base.

TACKLE AND TACTICS

The tackle used for red steenbras depends largely on the depth of the water in which you plan to fish. In shallow water (up to a depth of about 60 metres) a 15-kilogram-class boat rod and a matching reel that can hold approximately 200 metres of 15- or 24-kilogram line should be quite adequate. To fish in deeper water, especially in the current, a Scarborough reel is the best to use as it is difficult to set the hook when fishing for this species, and the fast retrieval rate of the Scarborough will allow the angler to wind on the fish. The trick is to get the fish off the bottom.

THE HOOK-UP

Once a red steenbras has taken the bait it will bore down to the bottom, and put up a strong fight but as soon as it leaves the bottom, especially in deep water, its air bladder starts to inflate in response to decreasing air pressure and this assists the angler in bringing the fish to the surface. At this point the fish's stomach is protruding from its mouth and, should the fish be undersized or out of season, the angler is faced with the dilemma of getting it back down to the bottom without harming it.

Some anglers are under the impression that in order to release such a baratruama species all that is required is to puncture the protruding stomach. This is not so: the fish must be unhooked and then the hook reinserted through the membrane of the dorsal fin or through the skin in front of the dorsal fin. The fish must then be carefully placed in the water, with the angler taking care that the hook does not tear out, and let down to the bottom. Once the fish is on the bottom, the hook can be released by the angler jerking the line (not the rod).

EATING QUALITY

Red steenbras is a much sought-after table fish. The flesh is excellent to eat, regardless of the size of fish.

RED STUMPNOSE
(Chrysoblephus gibbiceps)

Other common names: Miss Lucy (Port Elizabeth), Mighel (Knysna), *bonte dageraad* or *magistraat* (Struisbaai) and *rooi-witkop* (Hermanus).

DISTRIBUTION
The red stumpnose has a limited distribution, occurring only in the western, southern and eastern Cape from Cape Town to East London. It is essentially a cooler-water species and local availability is strongly influenced by the movement of cooler bottom water on to inshore reefs.

FEEDING HABITS
Red stumpnose are careful and deliberate bottom feeders and prefer calm, warm conditions. They feed mainly by puffing water out of their mouths, using their gill plates to 'blow' away coarse sand and shell grit in the small hollows of low profile reefs. In this manner they uncover various worms, crustaceans and molluscs. They have powerful jaws and it is said that they are also capable of ripping open young redbait pods with their teeth to get at the soft animal inside.

BAIT
Sea urchins, redbait, crabs and small fish make good bait, but a strip of squid, or a squid head when small fish are a nuisance, or a piece of cleaned or uncleaned leg of octopus are the best baits for red stumpnose.

(Whether one should or should not clean octopus leg when using it as bait is a debatable point and opinions offered are many and varied. I have not heard a conclusive argument for or against it and believe it is a matter of personal preference.)

WHERE TO CATCH

A sandy bottom with isolated flat reefs is good ground to drift over on a calm day. Good catches of red stumpnose are also made by boat anglers who are prepared to look for reefs away from the better-known angling grounds where the bigger fish are fond of feeding. The best catches are made along the stretch of coast between Cape Agulhas and Martha's Point near Arniston from summer through to late autumn, with February and March being the most productive months.

TACKLE AND TACTICS

As with most bottom feeders, light tackle produces the best catches on the inshore reefs as it allows you to present a natural-looking and enticing bait. A rod with a soft, sensitive tip and a reel filled with 6- or 8-kilogram line works very well because such a rig allows you to use a much lighter sinker to keep the bait on the bottom. A ball or barrel sinker sliding freely above the swivel, and a long hook trace with a 4/0 or

5/0 hook completes the terminal tackle.

Keep the bait on the bottom and your line slack: this is the secret of successful red stumpnose angling. Be prepared to lose a bit more tackle than the other anglers on board, especially if you are fishing on the drift. Ultimately, however, your success rate will more than reward you for the extra effort you have put into making up new traces.

THE HOOK-UP

Red stumpnose are quite shy and often mouth the bait without tugging on the line. The soft tip of the rod, however, will indicate that you have a fish sucking on the bait well before you feel any resistance. Lower the tip of the rod, take up the slack line and strike when next you feel the weight. This technique is also very successful with other bottom feeders such as *dageraad* and red roman.

Although it is said that the red stumpnose is not a good fighting fish, I beg to differ. On light tackle this fish gives a very good account of itself, as it is a stubborn fighter and not easy to get off the bottom.

EATING QUALITY

The flesh of the red stumpnose is soft, white, juicy and very tasty. When braaied it tastes very much like rock lobster.

SPOTTED GRUNTER
(Pomadasys commersonni)

DISTRIBUTION
The spotted grunter is a warm-water fish occuring along the entire east coast of Africa and as far south as False Bay.

FEEDING HABITS
Like the white steenbras, the spotted grunter likes the holes and channels in sandbanks and estuaries, where he uses a jet of water to blow small prey, such as mole crabs, white mussels and prawns from their holes.

BAIT
Although the best baits with which to catch this fish are those for which it forages, along the KwaZulu-Natal south coast spotted grunter are also caught on sardine (pilchard) during the annual sardine run.

WHERE TO CATCH
Along the southern Cape coast anglers catch most spotted grunter in the warm waters of estuaries during the summer months, while north of Port Elizabeth they are also caught in the sea close to river mouths. They are very skittish, and noise, especially in estuaries or quiet river stretches, will frighten them away.

Places such as St Lucia, Durban harbour and East London are well known for their annual spotted grunter runs. At St Lucia the grunter are normally most abundant in May and December, while the summer months can be particularly good in the southern Cape estuaries, especially in the Swartkops, Breede, Keurbooms and Bitou rivers.

TACKLE AND TACTICS

Spotted grunter are, by and large, light-tackle sportfish, although the odd specimen can be caught on conventional beach-fishing tackle in shallow, broken water in a bay. In estuaries and lagoons anglers using the lightest tackle possible produce excellent catches and also experience the game-fight of the spotted grunter to its fullest extent, similar to that offered by the white steenbras.

Many an angler, however, has spent a frustrating trip watching spotted grunter – heads down, their tails out of the water – foraging for prawns and worms and refusing to take any of the baits presented. When they are feeding like this they are not caught in great numbers but the occasional fish can be enticed by using a fly rod to cast a prawn bait in the mud cloud created by the water-pumping action of the grunter.

In rivers, spotted grunter can be caught from the bank but fishing from a small boat, using the same light tackle, produces the best results by far. Most anglers prefer to anchor the boat and wait for the shoal to reach them as the tide pushes in or runs out. A good technique to use on the incoming tide is to drift upriver with the tide, keeping a bait close to the bottom. This works well provided that the incoming tide does not make the water too clear.

Using a light graphite rod and a fixed-spool reel filled with 4-kilogram breaking-strain nylon, cast a prawn bait on a 1/0 hook in the direction of the pushing tide so that the bait, kept on the bottom with a small ball sinker, slowly follows the boat as you drift with the tide. An incoming tide at dawn or dusk normally produces the best catches. This technique can be very successful provided that the wind does not blow too strongly.

THE HOOK-UP

Like the white steenbras, once hooked a spotted grunter will fight to the bitter end. Boat anglers should remember to carry a landing net on board. Shore anglers must wait for the fish to be played out before it can be led to the beach.

EATING QUALITY

With flesh similar to that of the white steenbras, spotted grunter is excellent to eat as long as it is kept cool after it has been caught. A coolbox or damp hessian bag are ideal for storing fish, as your catch can very easily spoil if unprotected from the summer sun.

YELLOWTAIL
(Seriola lalandi)

DISTRIBUTION

Although most abundant in the vicinity of False Bay and Struisbaai, yellowtail are found from Port Nolloth on the west coast, where they are occasionally caught by boat anglers fishing for Cape snoek, to KwaZulu-Natal, where they are caught mostly during the annual sardine run.

Yellowtail undertake short migrations between the various reefs and banks. These are normally a response to wind changes and subsequent baitfish movement, which explains why yellowtail can be found at a certain spot one day but not the next.

Elsewhere in the world this species is found off the southern coast of Australia and the northern part of New Zealand, where they are known as yellowtail kingfish or kingie. Very large fish, weighing as much as 20 to 30 kilograms, can be caught there and with record-class specimens weighing 40 to 60 kilograms. In America, yellowtail are known as amberjack and can grow as large as 90 kilograms.

The average size of a Cape yellowtail caught in the shoals is usually between 3 and 5 kilograms, while loners or small-shoal yellowtail may grow to as much as 20 kilograms.

FEEDING HABITS

Yellowtail tend to congregate in shoals and feed mainly on small pelagic fish and squid, but they can be a frustrating fish for the angler to pursue as they are so unpredictable. They can often be seen swimming slowly on the surface yet they will show no interest in any lure or bait, no matter how well presented. (This is often the case in False Bay during September and October, when large shoals are seen but only a few fish are landed, and the odd fish that is taken is usually caught early in the morning or late in the afternoon.) On other occasions, fish that have not been biting all day suddenly move to the surface and start feeding frantically, striking at any lure or spinner the angler offers.

BAIT

Yellowtail are generally only responsive to bait when they are found beneath the surface – for instance, swimming around pinnacles. Then they will take strips of squid or a fish bait such as sardine (pilchard).

WHERE TO CATCH

From an angling point of view this fish species is unique. It is commonly caught from boats although anglers have developed specific methods to catch it from the shore. Nonetheless, both shore- and boat-fishing methods involve similar strategies.

Shore anglers Yellowtail are caught from rocky headlands where the water close inshore is deep, allowing the shoals to swim by within casting distance. In False Bay yellowtail are caught from the ledges at Rooikrans in the Cape Peninsula National Park, probably one of the most popular and well-known fishing spots in South Africa, and from the Rooiels ledges on the eastern side of False Bay. Yellowtail usually make their appearance at Rooikrans during September and are often caught until the following May. At Rooiels they are seldom caught at the beginning of summer but many are caught between February and April.

Further up the coast yellowtail are also caught by shore anglers from the Robberg peninsula at Plettenberg Bay, at Cape St Francis, Cape Recife, and Mazeppa Bay. However, the best and most consistent catches by shore anglers are made in False Bay at places such as Rooikrans and Rooiels.

When conditions are favourable, hundreds of boats congregate at Struisbaai, which has been the prime catching area for this species. Bird Island in Delagoa Bay has, in the past, also produced good catches.

In KwaZulu-Natal, yellowtail are caught by ski-boats on the Protea Bank.

TACKLE AND TACTICS
Catching yellowtail from the rocks
This is a highly specialized form of angling and starts with the selection of suitable tackle.

In earlier days, anglers would purchase a rod in the medium-tackle class and then take 10 or 12 centimetres off at the tip to stiffen the action of the rod. They reasoned that a stiff rod assisted in fighting the fish, as yellowtail are prone to dive for the nearest reef or the bottom, and also that it facilitated the lifting of the fish out of the water without the aid of a gaff. To catch a second fish out of a shoal, some anglers would keep a second rig ready and, having landed a yellowtail with the first rig, would put it to one side with the fish still on the hook and cast with the second.

To complement such a stiff rod, 18-kilogram breaking-strain line was used on a Penn 49 or 49A (probably the most popular of the all-purpose fishing reel during the '60s and '70s and still being used today by certain diehards).

The beginning of the 1980s, however, saw a change in strategy when spinnermen moved away from heavy tackle. Their catches had declined and they felt that by using lighter line and smaller spinners they could entice fish that normally would not strike on the heavier tackle.

Today, a quick-tapering rod (3- to 3,5-metres long) with a high-retrieval-rate reel such as a Shimano or Daiwa filled with 10- or 12-kilogram line are standard tackle. The lighter rod tip and line class make it possible for anglers to cast with lighter spinners, which in turn have a better action in the water.

Fishing from the shore for gamefish involves a group effort. Anglers normally take turns to sit high above the ledges, from where they spot approaching shoals and give casting directions to the anglers below. (Polarized sunglasses and a peaked cap are essential accessories for spotters, as they cut out the glare of the sun on the water and make spying the fish much easier.)

The art of casting a spinner ahead of and beyond a shoal of yellowtail, particularly in windy conditions, takes time to develop as one has to allow for the strength and direction of the wind. This is quite difficult at first but the more you practise the easier it becomes. Try to avoid landing your spinner on top of a shoal, as this normally causes the shoal to scatter and lessens the chances of hooking a fish. Conversely, once a yellowtail has been hooked, the rest of the shoal stays with the fighting fish and the other anglers can then cast a spinner or bait close to the hooked fish for extra catches.

Fishing from a boat While shore anglers fish for yellowtail from headlands and ledges, boat anglers search for them in the vicinity of undersea pinnacles, offshore reefs, islands, under drifting objects such as a mass of kelp or a large piece of wood, and by looking for birds hovering above a feeding shoal.

When a boat angler suspects that a shoal of yellowtail has congregated around a pinnacle of a reef, he will troll over that pinnacle. If this method is not successful the angler will stop close to the pinnacle and fish with drift lines baited with strips of squid or sardine cutlets.

A colour-video echosounder, used with a position-finding instrument such as the simple-to-operate Decca yacht navigator or a GPS (Global Positioning System), is a definite

The fight is over – a yellowtail is ready to be gaffed.

asset when fishing for yellowtail. Once a shoal has been observed on an echosounder the experienced skipper will enter the position of the shoal into his navigating instrument and then, each time the shoal stops biting, will move back to his original position above the pinnacle to pick up the shoal once again, which is likely to have regrouped around the pinnacle where he first located them. (Yellowtail seem to regroup and orientate themselves around pinnacles or other structures in the sea, such as an oil platform.)

At Struisbaai the recreational and commercial boat anglers catch most of their yellowtail on bait while fishing on banks such as Vlakbank, Blougansie and the Twelve Mile Bank. As a rule the boats never anchor but rather drift. The number of boats fishing on a bank such as Vlakbank, and the fact that boats of different sizes and shapes drift at different speeds often leads to chaotic fishing conditions. Anglers literally have to push boats apart to land their fish. Most of the fish are caught on handlines rigged with a small barrel sinker, the size of which depends on the strength of the current, and a large (10/0) hook baited with a strip of squid.

If there are only a few boats fishing on the bank, yellowtail can be caught by slowly trolling baited lines (see pages 178-180) and, once a fish is hooked, keeping it on the line while slowly circling. The rest of the shoal stays with the hooked fish and bites freely in the disturbed water caused by the circling boat.

Catching yellowtail with a spinner from a stationary boat can be very exciting. The sight of feeding gamefish churning up the water will cause even an experienced angler to tremble with excitement. When spinning for yellowtail the boat should be positioned upwind from the shoal to allow the angler to use the wind to cast the necessary distance. Your tackle is the conventional 3-metre rod and a multiplying reel with a smooth drag capable of 250 metres of 12- to 17-kilogram breaking-strain line; however, a wide range of spinners should be kept on hand, as the feeding habits of yellowtail are unpredictable, and while your normal selection may work well on most days, there are days when the fish favour a particular type or shape of spinner. On an overcast day, a dull spinner is likely to produce better results than the spinner you spent hours polishing to a shine the previous night.

The better spinner-fishermen develop the ability to focus on the shoal and cast from any conceivable position without being distracted by the activities of the other anglers.

This is a thrilling and most exciting part of yellowtail fishing, as the angler is casting at fish on the surface and actually watching them chase and grab his spinner.

THE HOOK-UP

Yellowtail are extremely strong fighters, and good tackle and skilful angling are required to bring this fish to the gaff. The experienced angler will not lift the rod to set the hook as soon as he feels a tug, but will continue winding in his spinner until he can hardly wind any more. Only when he feels something solid will he lift the rod to set the hook.

EATING QUALITY

Yellowtail is an excellent, firm-fleshed fish but due to overcooking is often regarded as dry. This is not so. Well basted, it is delicious cooked on a braai, or it can be poached, grilled, fried or baked. It is an excellent fish for pickling and freezes well.

A yellowtail landed from the well-known ledges at Rooikrans in the Cape Peninsula National Park.

CHAPTER EIGHT

DEEP-SEA BIG-GAME ANGLING

Deep-sea fishing is a relatively new sport in South Africa. Its origins go back to the late 1940s, when the first ski-boats were launched in the Bay of Natal to take the pioneer ski-boat anglers beyond the surf zone. In boats barely 5 metres long, and powered by outboards that were so slow that the boats could only be beached by paddling them shorewards with the bow facing the oncoming waves, those Durban anglers made outstanding catches of sailfish and marlin.

In the early 1950s the first Cape boat anglers started catching tuna off Cape Point, but their boats were large, sturdy, displacement-hull vessels capable of a top speed of 10 to 12 knots. However, fishing out of Simon's Town involved a total steaming time of seven to nine hours to the tuna grounds and back, which did not leave much time for fishing. To overcome this problem the boats needed to be capable of a much faster cruising speed, which meant a completely different hull design.

In the 1960s radical changes took place in the design of boats used by Cape deep-sea anglers and this ultimately led to the development of the 10- to 15-metre offshore boats which today are capable of achieving a top speed of close to 30 knots. These boats were (and still are) expensive to build, operate and maintain, and as a result not many Cape anglers participated in deep-sea angling until the ski-boat, so popular in Natal, made its appearance in Cape waters. With safer launching available from slipways, as opposed to the Natal launch through the surf, cabins were added to the design to provide anglers with some protection against the Cape weather. The ski-boat fleet expanded rapidly, and although the boats were small, deep-sea angling became more accessible to more anglers.

Present-day ski-boats can be anything up to 6,5 metres in length (some are larger) and usually have twin outboard motors and a comfortable, well-equipped fishing platform for the angler. Their level of sophistication, as far as electronic equipment is concerned, is on a par with the big boats. Fitted with a 29 MHz and VHF radio, colour echo-sounder, radar and an electronic navigating aid such as a GPS (global positioning system), they are capable of safely fishing up to 40 miles offshore.

The southern African coastline can be divided into three areas according to the species of gamefish caught off each:

SALDANHA BAY TO CAPE HANGKLIP

The surface water of this region is cooler than that of the rest of the eastern seaboard and the *longfin tuna*, a species that occurs worldwide, preferring surface temperatures in the range of 16 to 21 °C, predominates in this region. Although apparently over-exploited, longfin support the South African commercial pole fishery as well as a sport fishery. They are most abundant off Cape Point in the spring (before the water becomes too warm) and again in March, April and May.

Opposite: Sportfishing boats such as Lady Ella *are capable of achieving speeds of 25 knots or more, considerably shortening the travelling time between base and the offshore tuna-fishing grounds.*

Yellowfin tuna, once the prime target species of the Cape tuna fishermen, are no longer as abundant in local waters as they were some 30 years ago, when they were caught in large numbers within 20 miles of the coast. Today Cape tuna anglers are

Above: Longfin tuna (Thunnus alalunga).
Right: Yellowfin tuna (Thunnus albacares).
Below: Skipjack (Katsuwonus pelamis).

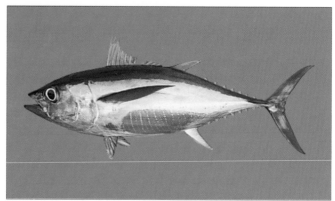

obliged to fish up to 40 miles offshore. However, the few shoals of large yellowfin (in the 40- to 60-kilogram class) that make their appearance during the summer months provide excellent sportfishing, as most anglers use much lighter tackle than the 36- and 54-kilogram rigs that were the norm when yellowfin fishing was at its best.

During the early days few Cape anglers made the effort to troll large lures for marlin; the excellent tuna catches spoilt them to such an extent that even though catches became smaller over the years, anglers were reluctant to troll large lures or baits for fear of missing out on the excitement that tuna provides.

Gamefishing tournaments offering large cash prizes for the biggest billfish caught played a significant role in changing the attitude of Cape deep-sea anglers. Once larger lures and baits were trolled, anglers found that marlin were far more abundant than they had realized, but although a number of boats report seeing and hooking marlin, only a few have been landed.

The most significant development in Cape gamefishing has been the founding of a sport fishery for *broadbill swordfish* to the exclusion of targeted commercial fishing. Broadbill (the name used by local anglers for the swordfish) is known worldwide as a prized angling fish and the high strike and hook-up rate has already attracted the attention of overseas gamefishermen.

There had always been an awareness of the presence of this species in Cape waters, as local deep-sea trawlers often used to catch broadbill in their trawl nets when fishing west of the Peninsula. However, as broadbill fishing entails spending the night at sea up to 40 miles offshore, there was no rush to develop the fishery. It was only when, after weeks of planning, two Cape anglers, Fergus Hamel and Nic de Kock, went to sea one Friday night in 1986 to fish specifically for swordfish, and returned the next morning with the first broadfill swordfish to be caught as a targeted fish, that local anglers took notice of the potential of this fishery. Since then broadbill fishing has become very popular and the annual tournament held off Cape Point attracts leading southern African as well as overseas deep-sea anglers.

Broadbill swordfish (Xiphias gladius).

The occurrence of broadbill swordfish is not limited to western Cape waters. Anglers fishing off Port Elizabeth have also been successful in landing this species, and I know of a small broadbill that was caught at night on a handline from a boat fairly far offshore from Durban.

Other species caught by Cape deep-sea anglers include dorado (especially at the height of summer when the water beyond the shelf edge is at its warmest), skipjack, mako shark and the occasional big-eye tuna. A few southern bluefin tuna have also been caught by anglers fishing for broadbill near the Good Hope Canyon.

CAPE HANGKLIP TO EAST LONDON

Although longfin tuna are occasionally caught between Cape Hangklip and Cape Agulhas, the variety of species in this region is influenced by the Agulhas current and the species caught are generally the warm-water game-fish such as **yellowfin tuna, skipjack, striped bonito** and **marlin.** Good catches of yellowfin tuna were made off Mossel Bay in earlier years, while the present-day hot spot seems to be at the edge of the Agulhas current off Jeffreys Bay and Port Elizabeth. Plettenberg Bay occasionally pro-duces a yellowfin run that provides excellent sport as the shoals move close inshore, within reach of all types of boats. I am told that one angler, fishing from an inflatable boat, hooked a yellowfin tuna close to Beacon Isle beach. He guided the tuna shorewards, beached his inflatable and fought the fish from the shore!

Throughout this region marlin are sighted, and occasionally hooked, but, as in the western Cape, few are landed. Anglers fishing for yellowtail off the banks at Struisbaai often report having sighted marlin or talk excitedly of how a marlin has rushed towards their boat to grab or spike a hooked yellowtail. It can therefore be only a matter of time before this gamefish becomes a targeted species

EAST LONDON TO MOZAMBIQUE

The closer one moves to the Mozambique border the better the billfishing becomes. As a result, big-game anglers fishing along this stretch of coast are well versed in the art of billfish trolling and baitfishing techniques. Anglers fishing out of Durban regularly catch billfish – usually *sailfish* and *marlin*, though *swordfish* have also been reported – while further north Sodwana has become the most popular billfish angling resort, where anglers can expect rather than hope to do battle with these supreme angling fish.

Striped marlin (Tetrapturus audax).

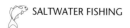

The continental shelf is very narrow along this part of the coast and gamefishermen fish close to the shore in near tropical conditions.

Sailfish, a spectacular gamefish to catch on light tackle, is one of the most commonly caught billfishes of this region. It occurs singly or in small shoals close to the surface and is caught on lures or trolled strips of fish bait.

FISHING CONDITIONS

Fishing conditions along the southern African coastline are often rough and, even when calm, are liable to change quite suddenly. In the **western Cape** the southeasterly gales that blow during the summer months, and the resultant upwelling that occurs along the coast, cool the water and boat anglers have to travel a long distance offshore before reaching a thermal front. Even then, conditions are normally not favourable for longfin tuna, as this species prefers the clear water that is found some distance beyond the thermal front. Yellowfin tuna may be found at the change and often bite late in the afternoon when the baitfish that occur here move to the surface.

During the autumn months light westerly or southwesterly winds prevail and create ideal conditions for tuna fishing. The warm water is pushed closer to the shore and the tuna tend to stay in a particular area. Longfin tuna can often be caught within an area of one or two square miles and will stay in the area provided conditions remain constant. Experienced anglers are aware of this behavioural pattern and punch the coordinates into their electronic navigating instrument, making it easy to return to the hot spot on subsequent fishing days.

While longfin tuna are known to come on the bite before a northwesterly blow, yellowfin tuna often bite well when the southeaster blows. Some of the best catches of yellowfin have been made when wind and spray as well as choppy, unpredictable seas, make fishing unpleasant. It is, however, remarkable how quickly anglers become oblivious to sea and weather conditions when they can see the fish feeding on the surface and the lures are grabbed as soon as they are let out behind the boat!

Fishing conditions along the **eastern Cape and KwaZulu-Natal** coastlines are somewhat different to those that prevail in the Western Cape. Apart from a few harbours where boats can put to sea in relatively calm conditions, there are very few bays or slipways where ski-boats can be launched without a fuss. In most cases boats are launched from the beach into the open sea and the skippers need to have experience to read the conditions in order to launch and beach their boats safely. The positions of sand bars and channels can change overnight, and visiting skippers should not attempt a beach launch if they are unfamiliar with the local sea and weather conditions. Rather be safe than sorry: visit the local boat club and ask for assistance or, if it can be arranged, have a local skipper accompany you.

As discussed previously, the configuration of the ski-boats that are launched through the surf differs markedly from that of boats that can be launched from a slipway. It is imperative that the former incorporate little or no super-structure in order to avoid resistance – and certain disaster – as the boat punches through the waves. (See page 141.)

Fishing conditions along the eastern seaboard are influenced by the easterly and westerly winds, which are known to change water conditions within an hour. The westerly winds are the worst, as they blow against the current making the swells steep and unpredictable. Fortunately the continental shelf is narrow between Port Elizabeth and the Mozambican border and most of the boat fishing takes place relatively close to the shore. Danger arises when boats are fishing well into the current and have to travel across the current, beam on, to reach the safety of the shore.

Boat angling in southern African waters tests not only the angling ability of boat fishermen but also the boat-handling and navigational skills of the skippers. It is to the

credit of the boat-angling clubs and provincial bodies that they have an excellent safety record. No recreational boats may put to sea without the skipper having successfully completed his skipper's ticket. The course, offered under the auspices of the South African Deep-Sea Angling Association (SADSAA), is approved by the marine division of the Department of Transport. The SADSAA safety officers, along with the above-mentioned government department, also ensure that uniform safety regulations, applicable to all small craft, are strictly adhered to. Each year the accredited safety officers inspect all the affiliated boats before issuing them with safety certificates.

FINDING THE FISH

There are a number of places in which gamefish shoals can be found. These include water with the appropriate temperature and colour; in the vicinity of current lines, banks and reefs; along the migratory path of pelagic baitfish shoals; around structures and drifting objects; in the vicinity of commercial trawlers, and where hovering sea birds give away their location.

Seabirds often give away the position of gamefish shoals by circling the area, hovering or just rafting on the water.

Successful gamefishing is a team effort. The boat that consistently catches the most fish is one where the entire crew is involved, helping to find the target by looking for the signs that indicate the presence of gamefish, and by making full use of any available electronic equipment to locate shoals beneath the surface and to plot their position or the direction in which they are moving. Successful anglers understand the behaviour of their target species and the conditions that influence their behaviour, and although conditions may differ in what seem to be only small, insignificant ways each day, experienced anglers are able to interpret these changes and instinctively end up where the best catches can be made.

Keep a record of the water temperature in which you catch your target species, as this helps you to develop a feel for the most favourable conditions. Remember that gamefish often feed in the morning and go off the bite at midday only to appear again in the late afternoon.

During March and April the demersal trawlers operating out of Cape Town and Saldanha Bay fish on the trawling grounds 25 to 30 miles offshore between Hout Bay and Cape Point. These boats are factory trawlers and process their catches on board. Offal and species that have no commercial value are dumped overboard and this creates an enormous chum slick which attracts not only gamefish such as yellowfin and longfin tuna but also thousands of sea birds – Cape gannets, whitechinned petrels, shy black-browed and yellownosed albatrosses, pintado petrels, sooty shearwaters and the smaller species such as terns and Wilson's storm petrel. Sharks and seals are also present and are part of the hectic feeding activities behind the trawlers.

Sea birds, when they are not scavenging around boats, often betray the presence of gamefish. Albatrosses and whitechinned petrels will circle over gamefish, waiting for them to rise to the surface, while Cape gannets and terns hover above the shoal, waiting for baitfish to be driven to

the surface. Gamefishing can be extremely tiring if there are no fish striking but anglers who remain alert will notice any distant bird activity or sudden disturbance of water when feeding gamefish break the surface.

GAMEFISHING METHODS

Gamefish can be caught by trolling with lures, trolling baits, drifting with baits, fishing with baits from a boat on anchor and casting lures like spinners and flies from a drifting or anchored boat. In recent times fly-fishing for gamefish has become very popular. In fact, a South African angler has established a world record for longfin tuna in the 8-kilogram tippet class.

With the exception of broadbill, which are caught at night, all gamefish are attracted to lures. Whether they take, however, depends on their feeding mood at the time. Spinning for gamefish is an alternative to trolling lures and is the method adopted either when the fish are reluctant to take lures, or as a second method after the boat has stopped to land gamefish such as tuna that have been hooked on lines.

LURE FISHING
Most experienced deep-sea anglers have their own opinion as to why lures work. Some say that gamefish strike at lures thinking they are some sort of food, while others maintain that the lures excite or annoy them. Whatever the reason, the presentation of a lure is most important as it is intrinsic to the deception you are trying to achieve.

Strategy A lure that works well behind a particular boat may be completely unsuccessful on a different boat on the same day. Why? While there is no simple answer to this question, there are many factors that need to be considered. The shape of the hull of the boat is important, as this may affect the size and the shape of the wake, which

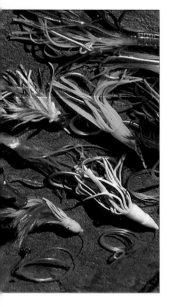

Some popular tuna fishing lures.

in turn will make the lure more or less visible. The engine and propeller noise or a vibration on a shaft may attract or frighten fish. The trolling speed must be considered, as some lures have a better action at a specific speed and very few boats troll at exactly the same speed.

The manner in which a lure has been assembled will also play a part, as the hole through the head of the lure may differ from one lure to another and may affect its swimming action. Whether a lure is trolled in an upright or a flat position will affect your success too, as some lures have a better swimming action when trolled on the surface while others work better when swimming deeper in the water. Success or failure may equally depend on the formation in which the lures are being trolled: close to the boat on the outside of the wake, in the middle of the wake or just behind it. The number of hooks, or the thickness or type of material from which the trace is made (wire or nylon) may also influence the swimming action of a lure.

The time of day and extent of cloud cover are just two of many aspects that play a role in the choice of lure. Experienced anglers will tell you that it is best to use a dark lure on a dull day. Blue or black lures with a touch of red or pink are very popular under these conditions. Remember, however, that what you read in books and magazines, or what other anglers tell you about lures and colour selection should be treated as guidelines only and should not deter you from being innovative. The large catches of gamefish that were not uncommon some years ago are now the exception rather than the rule and to remain at the head of the class you need to be innovative and alert.

NOTE

* Surface lures appeal to a broad cross-section of species and allow you to cover large distances in good time as they can be trolled much faster than a bait or subsurface lure. Experiment with combinations of lure types. Deep-swimming lures often work well on the outer trolling positions, while trolling some lures flat and some in an upright position adds variety and action to the lures, particularly on a calm day.

* When you come across a shoal of gamefish feeding on the surface, avoid trolling through the shoal as this is likely to scare the fish and cause them to scatter and dive. Steer the boat parallel to the shoal and once past, turn to allow the lures to run through the spot where the shoal is feeding.

Through the years the most popular lure colour combinations have been red and white, blue and white, red and blue, and green and yellow. A few years ago no Cape deep-sea angler would have gone to sea without a variety of green and lime-green lures in his tackle box, as these were the colours that longfin tuna preferred. In contrast, the pioneer Cape tuna anglers would tell you that you could put out any lure you liked as long as it was red and white!

Subsurface lures Lures such as the Rapala type produce consistent results and can be used for practically any predatory species. These lures are made in a large selection of colours, although the so-called 'redhead' seems to be the most successful, no matter where you fish.

The shape, size and angle of the metal plate on the wobbling type of lure certainly influence the action of the lure. The further you bend it downwards, the greater the resistance through the water and the shallower the lure will run. Rapalas and their equivalents on the market are tank-tested and should swim properly when first used, but the angle of the metal plate (the lip) can very easily be disturbed by a fish grabbing it or by the angler leaving a fish with the lure in its mouth to thrash about on the deck.

A wobbling lure that is not swimming properly can cause chaos with its two sets of treble hooks. Once such a lure has jumped across another line and become tangled in it you need to get the tangle out of the wake as soon as possible. With light line it is often easier and safer to cut off the tangled lines and to redo the double lines and traces.

To retune a Rapala often requires a minor adjustment to the lip. This exercise may be very frustrating as it is easy to over-correct. Ask an expert to demonstrate the correct technique.

To sum up, always remember to choose a trolling pattern that is least likely to cause tangles, the pattern often being dependent on the state of the sea and the strength of the wind. Select your lures according to the prevailing weather conditions. Experiment with different lures when fish are reluctant to strike. If you are still not successful, adjust the trolling speed. Keep your hooks sharp, especially when using light tackle.

BAITFISHING

Trolling Provided that the tackle being used has been carefully prepared and that everyone on board does the right thing at the right time when the fish is brought alongside, trolling dead or live baits (usually skipjack, small yellowtail and tuna, mullet and large shad) for billfish can be both rewarding and exciting .

The importance of quality tackle and careful tackle preparation and maintenance cannot be over-emphasized. Billfish can test your tackle to the extreme and any shortfall in your gear preparation is bound to be exposed. Fishing for marlin and other billfish often involves hours of unproductive trolling and it is unforgivable for an angler to lose a fish as a result of line failure or a poorly tied knot.

Big-game fishing is normally associated with blue water and this often results in obvious hot spots, such as a current line, being ignored in the haste to get to the oceanic waters. Smaller gamefish species as well as juvenile yellowfin and longfin tuna often feed on the baitfish that occur on the current line, and although the water may be warm, the colour could be green or blue-green – not the colours normally associated with gamefish. Skipjack and juvenile yellowfin tuna can normally be seen on the surface and, as they are the natural prey of marlin, trolling one that you have caught on the day and stored in a cool-box to retain its natural colours and smell could be very profitable. Most skippers prefer to troll two baits, one in each outrigger, although when conditions are suitable it is quite possible to troll an additional bait from the middle trolling position.

There are many methods used to rig a live or dead bait for trolling. The following illustrations are a few of the more popular methods.

Dorado are spectacular gamefish to catch, especially on light line. The author's son, Gavin, is seen here with his South African junior record caught on 6-kilogram line.

DEAD-BAIT TROLLING

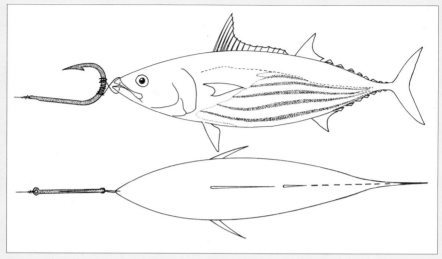

Bridle rig for live- or dead-bait trolling

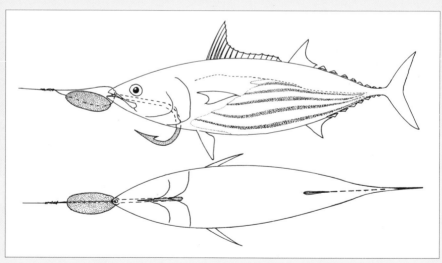

Oval sinker rig

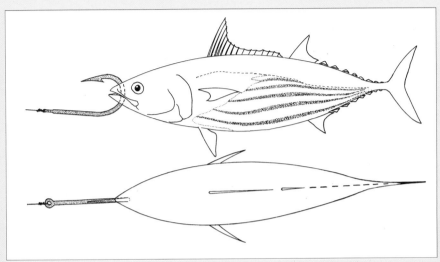

Catalina rig

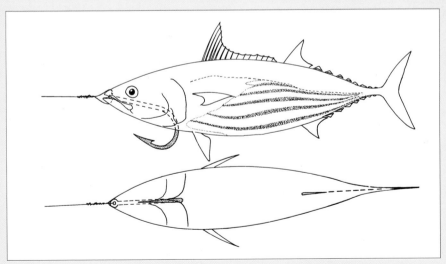

Single hook rig

Live-bait trolling

NOTE *When trolling, be sure to use a swivel, and make sure that it is functioning properly. Trolling without a swivel or with a frozen or seized swivel will result in the line becoming twisted, and a badly twisted line is very difficult to rewind on to the reel. If this should happen, cut the terminal tackle off and stream the line behind the boat while it is moving slowly ahead. Leave it out for a while and the line will untwist itself.*

The hook-up Regardless of which rig the angler uses, the baits should be fed into the water while the boat moves slowly ahead and, once the required length of line has been let out, the line should be clipped into the outrigger clip and hauled to the tip of the outrigger. The clip is held in position by securing the outrigger halyard in a cleat.

At this stage the angler on strike should have his harness and glove ready and he should be near the rod in order to be able to free-spool to 'feed' the fish more line or tighten the drag when the hook has to be set. If, for example, a marlin has investigated the bait but refuses to take it, feeding it more line might entice it to grab the bait. Once enough line has been fed and the angler judges that the bait has been swallowed, the skipper should open the throttles and keep the boat on a straight course while the angler on strike retrieves the slack line and strikes to set the hook. The striking drag should be a third of the breaking strain of the line and once the fish is hooked the drag setting can be increased to half the breaking strain.

As soon as a fish has been hooked the other lines should be wound in as quickly as possible and the deck should be cleared of all unnecessary items that could get in the way while the fish is fought or when it is brought to the gaff. Many a record fish has been lost at the side of the boat when it was ready to be gaffed, and the chances of this happening will be greatly reduced if everybody has a specific task and is ready to do it. One crew member should take the trace while another should stand by with the gaff. The flying gaff should be secured to a sturdy cleat and the rope should be long enough to reach either side of the boat. The fish should be gaffed in the head or shoulder and the gaffer should then pull the gaff handle free so that all the strain goes on to the rope. A tail rope should then be secured to immobilize the fish.

Small billfish that are going to be released can be grabbed by the bill and held while the hook is cut loose and, if available, a tag inserted. (For information on tag and release, see page 229.)

Grabbing the trace is possibly the most dangerous task to perform. Remember to feed the retrieved trace back overboard to keep it from tangling or, even worse, looping around limbs of the angler.

DRIFT FISHING FOR BROADBILL SWORDFISH

Broadbill fishing is a very new facet of big-game angling in southern African waters. Although the first broadbill was caught as recently as 1986 and received wide publicity, it took another four years before the next one was landed. After a period of good fishing, catches started to dwindle almost overnight as a result of the commercial exploitation of this source. During the peak season (late 1980s and early 1990s) catches were published in popular angling magazines and the Cape was widely known as a good fishing spot for broadbill. The Good Hope Canyon at Cape Point was one of the most productive angling spots along the entire coastline. The following extract from Nic de Kock's article, 'Broadbill Bonanza', which appeared in the magazine *Ski-boat* after the first broadbill competition, relates how hectic the action can become: 'Between the hours of seven o'clock and one o'clock the next morning the fleet (six boats) recorded a staggering 13 suspected broadbill strikes with four fish being boated and three being lost near the boat after positive identification! One boat reported four hook-ups with one fish boated.'

Strategy Broadbill are caught at night by drifting with rigs baited with large squid. To cover the most productive depths three lines are lowered to different depths, between 10 and 150 metres from the surface. Positioning the bait at a specific depth is not as easy as it sounds as wind, current and the speed at which a boat is drifting under the prevailing conditions makes this task very diffi-cult. Ideally you should end up with a shallow, a mid-depth and a deep bait.

The shallow and mid-depth lines are let out first and each is held at the selected depth by means of a balloon, which can be tied to the main line with dental floss. Some anglers place a lightstick in the balloon to keep track of its position. The deepest line can be let down alongside the boat. By lowering the shallower lines first and spreading them over a depth range, the likelihood of the lines becoming tangled is greatly reduced.

Although a number of broadbill swordfish have been landed on tackle lighter than 24-kilogram breaking strain, the general consensus is that 36-kilogram tackle, or heavier, is the most appropriate to use, for sooner or later someone is bound to end up battling with a really large specimen that may simply be too strong and heavy for lighter tackle.

Preparing the bait Broadbills are caught on rigs which have been baited with squid and prepared before going to sea. The squid should be removed from the deepfreeze and left until soft enough for the hooks to be inserted. It is advisable to prepare as many as 20 baits at a time. Once rigged, the baits, complete with hooks and traces, are individually wrapped and refrozen.

The recommended hook sizes are 10/0 to 12/0 for the upper hook and 11/0 to 13/0 for the lower hook. Each hook of the double-hook rig should be enlarged by wrapping electrical tape around the shank and the bend; dental floss is then tied around the tape to stop it from unravelling. Broadbill swordfish have very soft mouths and anglers tape up the hooks to enlarge them, in the belief that the larger and softer the surface area of the hook is, the less prone it is to tearing out.

The two hooks are rigged on a 100- or 150-kilogram nylon trace which is fed through the body cavity of the squid to position the hooks inside, with the bend and the tip of each hook exposed. The squid is then sewn on to the trace to prevent it from sliding down and forming a lump on the hooks. Next, the nylon trace is attached to a heavy-duty gamefish swivel, which in turn is attached to a second nylon trace. The rig is completed by attaching a breakaway sinker and a lightstick to the swivel.

The hook-up As with most baitfishing, when fishing for broadbill swordfish the angler should have his reel in freespool. As soon as he feels something taking the bait, he should feed enough line to enable the fish to take the bait properly before he strikes. Once a broadbill has been hooked, the angler should endeavour to get some 'sea room' between him and the fish; this can be done by asking the skipper to 'run away' from the fish to ensure that it does not swim too close to the boat too soon after being

Trolling rods from an upright position gives lures a more lively action, especially on a calm day.

hooked, when it is still 'green'. It is at this stage that most fish are lost, especially when they dive under the boat.

Broadbill swordfish are extremely strong fighters and, as many anglers have discovered, difficult to fight on a stand-up rig or without a fighting chair. After the angler has exhausted himself subduing the fish, it can be lost at the side of the boat as a result of inexperience or the crew simply not reacting fast enough.

Flying gaffs, tail ropes and gloves are all items that must be close at hand, and every person on board should know what he has to do to ensure that the entire tracing and gaffing (or tagging) operation is carried out as smoothly and as quickly as possible.

Whether to have the deck lights on while fishing at night or whether a spotlight should be held on a hooked fish has been widely debated. Some boats have hooked broadbill while the anglers were still feeding the line into the water, and all the deck lights were on. It may be that broadbill are attracted to a boat's lights. Trawlers drift at night and as there is always the chance of their finding fish offal around a trawler, these fish may expect to find the same around any other boat. To put a spotlight on a freshly hooked ('green') broadbill could be a foolish thing to do, as it may startle the fish, making it very difficult for the angler to get it to the boat.

BAIT FISHING FOR TUNA

Most of the early catches of tuna made by Cape sportfish-ermen were made by trolling surface lures, while the odd large yellowfin tuna was caught on bait, though this was the exception rather than the rule. However, among these sportfishermen were anglers who had learnt their game-fishing skills spinning for yellowtail off the rocks at Rooikrans. Soon spinning for tuna became popular among a small group of anglers who were willing to take the punishment of fighting yellowfin tuna well in excess of 40 kilograms on a 2,8-metre spinning rod and a Penn 49!

In the 1970s Brian Cohen, a prominent angler and one of the pioneers of commercial tuna fishing, brought a small American pole-fishing boat, *Maine*, to Simon's Town. It was only then that the practice of chumming and bait-fishing for tuna became entrenched. Soon boats were taking boxes of sardines (pilchards) to sea to use as chum and bait, and where previously the boats would continue trolling after the first longfin tuna had struck, in the hope of getting a full house, the skipper now turned in the direction of the strike and stopped the boat as soon as possible. While this was happening, pieces of chum would be thrown into the water to attract the shoal to the boat.

This method is now part of the tuna-fishing technique used by anglers between Saldanha Bay and Cape Hangklip, as it has proved especially successful for catching longfin tuna. In fact, nowadays it is unthought-of to go tuna-fishing off the Cape Peninsula without a few 5-kilogram boxes of sardines to use as bait.

On the way out to the tuna grounds it is the duty of one of the crew members (normally the most junior!) to prepare the chum and the bait. This is done by thawing out a box of bait and cutting the sardines into small blocks, which are then thrown into a bucket. On some, the tail portion (approximately 10 centimetres in length) is cut off and kept to one side as bait. Throughout the day the chum bucket is kept full and this generates a considerable amount of blood and oil.

Early in the Cape tuna season (October and November), tuna feed on the shoals of pelagic baitfish that are on their return journey from the west coast to the Agulhas Bank. During this time the tuna are often found beneath a gathering of birds and, although they may be taken on lures trolled behind the boat, they very seldom stay around a boat once a hooked fish has been brought to the gaff. Later in the season (towards the end of February and through March and April, when the shoals of anchovies have disappeared), once a longfin has been hooked on the

troll the rest of the shoal will follow it to the boat, looking for something to eat. By having a bucket of chum ready and tossing a few pieces into the water as soon as the boat slows down, the shoal can be attracted to the boat and, depending on the skill of the crew, the fish can be kept around the boat for a considerable length of time.

Baitfishing traces The breaking strain of the nylon trace depends on the size of the fish and whether or not they are reluctant to take the bait; shy fish can often be convinced to take the bait on a thinner trace. The size of the hook depends on whether you are catching yellowfin or longfin tuna: short-shank hooks are ideal to use, as you can hide the hook in a small piece of bait when the fish are shy.

Strategy When fish are hooked on the troll, the wheel-man puts the throttles into neutral and the boat slows down and finally stops side-on to the wind. As soon as the boat slows, a few pieces of chum are thrown into the water to attract the shoal to the boat. Some crew members will cast spinners, which is both a very productive and exciting way to catch tuna and draws the shoal towards the boat,

Well-equipped ski-boats are quite capable of fishing the offshore tuna grounds alongside larger sportfishing boats.

keeping the fish on the bite. Other crew members will attach a bait trace, consisting of a short (approximately 1,5-metre) trace and a short-shank bait hook, to their trolling tackle and bait up with the tail portions.

While the boat is drifting, the fish are kept near the boat by the crew throwing two or three pieces of chum into the water on the leeward side. Not too many pieces of chum should be thrown in at a time, as the fish will follow the chum as it drifts away and may then lose contact with the boat.

As soon as the longfin start feeding on the chum the bait traces can be put into the water. Longfin tuna glide into the slick with their pectoral fins fully extended and when they are on the bite their dorsal surface seems to be darker than normal. This is a very exciting way of catching tuna as sometimes you can actually feed the bait to the fish you wish to catch. Large yellowfin tuna quite often appear in the chum slick and add to the excitement. Feeding a whole sardine bait to such a large fish and watching it take the bait a few metres away from you really gets the adrenalin pumping.

In order to keep the shoal near the boat and feeding it is imperative that one or two anglers continue to spin, because the spinner as well as the hooked fish will keep the rest of the shoal interested and on the bite.

SPINNING OR SPOON-FISHING FOR TUNA
Tuna can be caught by casting a spinner at a shoal feeding on the surface; spinning blindly as a fish strikes on the troll; or working the chum slick. All types of surface-lure fishing are exciting, as most often the angler can see the action taking place. Spinning or spoon-fishing takes this one step further, as by slowing down or speeding up the retrieval rate, or changing the angle at which the rod is being held, the action of the spinner can be changed, enticing fish that are reluctant to strike. Often the shoal or a few fish will follow the spinner from the end of the cast

The author with a 60-kilogram, sickle-finned yellowfin tuna, caught west of Hout Bay on 24-kilogram line and stand-up tackle.

and will grab it only at the side of the boat. To see the entire event happening on the surface, from the time the fish start chasing the spinner until one fish rushes forward to grab it before the rest of the shoal can reach it, is, to my mind, the most exciting form of gamefishing. The thrill when your rod doubles over and the line starts peeling off your reel is truly something to experience.

Longfin tuna Although longfin do not grow as large as yellowfin tuna, the pace at which longfin can be caught when they are on the bite makes spinning for them hectic and exciting angling.

As soon as a longfin has been hooked on the troll, an angler may cast his spinner close to where the fish has struck (while the boat is slowing down) and, by hooking a fish or merely retrieving his spinner, he is likely to attract the rest of the shoal to the boat. By this time the first pieces of chum are already in the water. Once the boat has stopped and an oily chum slick has been created, tuna can be caught by casting the spinner up the slick and allowing it to sink below the surface before winding it back.

Yellowfin tuna This species can be caught either on a spinner (spoon) by casting at a shoal feeding on the surface or, in the way most of the longfin are caught, when the boat is drifting and a chum slick has been created. However, unlike longfin tuna, yellowfin are less likely to be attracted to a chum slick once one of them has been hooked on the troll.

The most exciting way, of course, is to cast a spinner into the feeding shoal. Yellowfin tuna often feed when fishing conditions are at their worst. Choppy seas and strong winds make casting very difficult, but such conditions are even more taxing for the skipper, who has to position the boat close to the shoal (within catching distance) while the shoal is moving at 10 knots per hour or more, and usually into the wind!

The angler must maintain his balance, watch his back cast (to avoid hooking one of the other anglers) and gauge his distance from the shoal and how far ahead of the shoal he will need to cast to allow for the speed at which the fish are travelling. Once the yellowfin start chasing the spinner – their backs out of the water – the excitement begins, but equally, once the spinner has been grabbed the hard work begins.

Unquestionably, yellowfin provide the tuna spinner-fisherman with the ultimate challenge. The fish frequently exceed 40 kilograms in weight, and the fight often ends up being extremely hard work. When fighting such a large fish on a 2,9-metre casting rod, with a reel in the class of a Shimano 20/40, standing up and without the aid of a harness, the angler takes the full strain. The fight may last as long as an hour and a half, and many an angler after landing his first yellowfin of over 50 kilograms on a spinner refuses ever to cast at them again!

Spinning tactics It is difficult to recommend a particular type of spinner. Most spinnermen have a few favourite spinners in which they have confidence and they will use them no matter what. Longfin tuna are often caught deeper down than are yellowfin, so a fairly heavy spinner will get you into action quicker than a lighter one. Your choice of spinner on any particular day may depend on the state of the sea, the wind and the weather, the class of tackle you are using and the type and size of baitfish that the tuna are disgorging on deck. Again, keep in mind that a dull brass spinner may give you more success on a dull, overcast day than a heavily-shined one.

The speed at which you retrieve a spinner depends on a number of factors, but before you start adjusting your retrieval speed to suit the conditions or the behaviour of the fish, you need to find the best retrieval rate for your set of tackle. Your best retrieval rate depends largely on the gear ratio of your reel and the shape and size of your spinner, but only with practice and experience will you arrive at the retrieval rate that gives your spinner the most natural action as it swims through the water.

The depth to which you let your spinner sink will depend on the behaviour of the fish. Sometimes they take the spinner close to the surface, while on other occasions you may have to let your spinner sink quite deep before winding it back. If you are no longer enticing the fish, change your tactics. Try letting your spinner sink deeper or next to the boat; cast a bit further, even beyond the edge of the chum slick, and bring the spinner back on the surface. Tuna, especially-longfin, often take the spinner while it is still sinking.

One final word of advice: remember to check the oval clips or rings that attach the hooks to the spinner, as they are prone to open up if you have been twisting or pulling the spinner out of the fishes' mouths. Also, take great care when you bring a fish alongside the boat – a spinner can be very dangerous should it pull out of a fish's mouth unexpectedly. Try to hold your rod at an angle pointing away from the other anglers. This will lessen the chance of their being hit.

Outstanding catches of longfin tuna are still made off the Cape Peninsula. Individual specimens weighing in excess of 25 kilograms are not uncommon.

CHAPTER NINE

MAPS AND AREA GUIDES

Doringbaai – one of only two protected inlets between Port Nolloth and Lamberts Bay.

THE CAPE

Stretching from the Orange River in the west to the KwaZulu-Natal border in the east, the coastal waters of the Cape offer anglers a range of species.

Along the narrow continental shelf of the east coast the warm Agulhas current flows strongly. This is a region noted for its rock and surf fishing and its many fine estuaries, where the warm water makes for good fishing throughout the year.

At Cape Agulhas the continental shelf widens considerably, extending approximately 100 nautical miles at its widest point. Here the warm water and rocky banks and reefs provide some of the finest fishing to be found along the entire Cape coastline, with plenty of species to satisfy both shore and boat angler.

West of Cape Agulhas the water starts to cool and kelp beds, which create calmer water conditions inshore, are found from here to Port Nolloth in almost all the nearshore rocky areas.

North of Cape Town the cold but nutrient-rich Benguela current, which flows along the west coast, brings its influence to bear on climate and vegetation. Despite its barrenness, this flat coastal plain has its own appeal, and the sea rewards local anglers with sizable catches, if not with a wide variety of species.

PORT NOLLOTH TO DORINGBAAI

This region is part of the arid west coast and, being so close to the Namib Desert, is very flat. While the winter vegetation and the springtime show of wildflowers attract visitors from all over the country, the summer months are dry and dusty and are not the ideal time to plan a visit. In contrast, the autumn months are characterized by cold fog banks that roll in from the sea on most nights – but usually clear by noon the following day. Although this is a long stretch of coastline, access is limited, as between Port Nolloth and Doringbaai diamonds are recovered from the sea and coastal plain.

Port Nolloth, a shallow natural harbour protected from the open sea by reefs, is the holiday resort of the diamond area. Rock lobster and diamond-dredging vessels operate out of this harbour, as do a few inshore trawlers. There is a hotel and a campsite in the village and a few beach bungalows at McDougal Bay, a few kilometres to the south.

The cold water of the Benguela current limits the number of species one can expect to catch along this coastline. Hottentot, galjoen (during the winter months) and white steenbras are the species most commonly caught. Shore anglers fish off sandy beaches or in the vicinity of rocks where there is a clear space in the kelp beds.

The commercial rock-lobster boats and 'bakkies' (rowing dinghies) make good catches of snoek during the autumn and early winter months, and enthusiastic snoek fishermen can easily arrange to accompany one of these boats.

195

Moving down the coast, **Hondeklipbaai** is the next place that offers commercial boats some protection against the rough winter seas, and a small village has developed around the rock lobster processing factory that is situated here. However, apart from the local general dealer and a campsite there are no facilities for visitors.

Galjoen and white steenbras can be caught from the sandy beaches when conditions are suitable, while hottentot are caught from the rocks by fishing into holes in the kelp beds.

Strandfontein is a seaside resort just south of the Olifants River mouth and is probably the most popular holiday centre of the Sandveld. The tarred road from the N7 to Strandfontein and **Doringbaai**, a rock-lobster fishing village a few kilometres south of Strandfontein, takes you through vineyards on either side of the Olifants River and past local co-ops where good-quality wines can be purchased. The alternative route, a gravel road between Lambert's Bay and Doringbaai, is well worth travelling during spring when the wild flowers are at their best.

As far as fishing is concerned, there are numerous rocky ledges and small bays between Strandfontein and Doringbaai where anglers catch hottentot and galjoen. Look for openings in the kelp to cast your bait, or fish in the white, foamy water close to reefs or rocky outcrops. White steenbras are caught along the sandy beaches to the south and north of Strandfontein.

LAMBERTS BAY TO CAPE COLUMBINE

Moving south from the Olifants River, **Lamberts Bay** is the first safe harbour for commercial fishing boats. The village owes its existence to the presence of a factory that processes pelagic fish (mainly anchovies) into fishmeal and packs rock-lobster products for the local and export markets.

Apart from the activity in the harbour, Bird Island, which is an integral part of the harbour and is joined to the mainland by a harbour wall, attracts many visitors who come to view the sea birds, such as Cape gannets and cormorants, that roost and breed here.

The harbour offers safe launching for small boats, and good catches of snoek can be made here during the winter months. Hottentot are caught from the boats when the snoek shoals are not around, while yellowtail are occasionally caught among the snoek.

Shore anglers catch hottentot during the summer months and during winter reasonable catches of galjoen can be made along the beach to the north of the village. The rocky coastline to the south of the village as well as the beach beyond are also good spots to fish for galjoen.

The small west coast village of **Elandsbaai** is probably better known for its surf, but it is well worth visiting as it is one of the west coast's white mussel hot spots. This quiet village has one small hotel and a caravan/campsite, all situated close to the beach.

During the winter months anglers travel along the beach in four-wheel-drive vehicles to look for the holes where galjoen are likely to be feeding. Baboon Point is a good spot to fish if you do not have a beach vehicle.

Verlorenvlei runs into the sea close to Baboon Point. The vlei is shallow but is well stocked with carp and certainly well worth visiting, especially if you are a fresh-water angler suffering from withdrawal symptoms.

St Helena Bay is a calm bay and the focal point of the west coast's

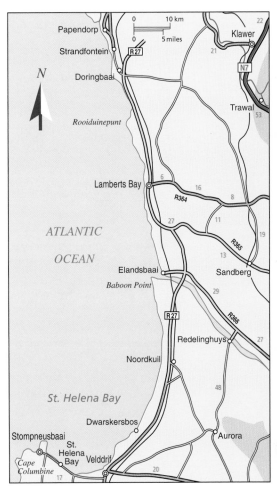

pelagic fishing industry. The pelagic fish, on their migratory path back to the Agulhas Bank, seem to extend their stay in the plankton-rich waters of the bay and hundreds of tons of anchovy, redeye and pilchard (for the canneries) are caught each night when the weather and fishing conditions are suitable. Anchovy and redeye are made into fishmeal and visitors to St Helena Bay will know when they are getting close to the village as the smell of the fishmeal plants is unmistakable!

Shoals of snoek feed on the pelagic fish and are caught in the bay during the early winter months. The annual snoek run attracts hundreds of snoek fishermen and, needless to say, accommodation is nearly impossible to find at the height of the run.

Shore anglers fish for galjoen during the winter months, while light-tackle enthusiasts can travel the short distance to **Velddrif** to fish for shad and white steenbras near the mouth of the Berg River.

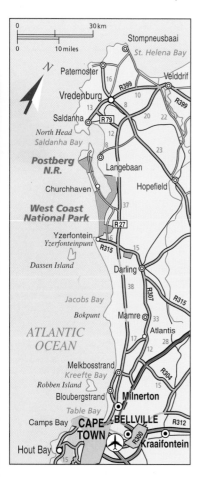

SALDANHA BAY TO CAPE TOWN

Saldanha Bay and **Langebaan Lagoon** offer safe and productive angling where the light-tackle boat enthusiast can enjoy fishing for species such as kob, white steenbras, white stumpnose, shad and various species of skate, ray and shark during the summer months. Most of these species may also be caught from the shore of the lagoon and close to the iron-ore jetty. Access to fishing spots outside the bay is limited, although galjoen and hottentot are caught along the rocky shoreline between North Head and Jacobs Bay.

Yzerfontein is a small holiday village very popular with ski-boat fishermen, as the slipway, although exposed and often difficult to launch from, facilitates fishing the grounds around **Dassen Island**. For some reason the snoek shoals that normally move past this area during the winter months reappear off

Dassen Island during the summer months, much to the delight of the Cape and west coast ski-boat snoek fishermen. During the winter months local residents catch galjoen and hottentot off the rocks close to the village.

Between Yzerfontein and Cape Town are the residential areas of **Melkbosstrand, Bloubergstrand** and **Milnerton**. The beaches between Milnerton and Melkbosstrand were once known for the excellent catches of galjoen that were made there by surf anglers during the Cape winter months. Urban development and easier access have changed this and today anglers battle to make even reasonable catches. At Kreefte Bay, between Bloubergstrand and Melkbosstrand, white steenbras are occasionally caught, while kob come on the bite during the winter months, particularly after an unseasonal southeasterly blow. **Table Bay harbour** is another fishing spot that no longer produces the excellent catches of hake, mackerel, maasbanker, skate and ray that were made off the East Pier and at A Berth during the '50s and '60s. Despite this, dedicated pier anglers still gather to fish here. (Permits for this area are issued only to members of angling clubs that are affiliated to the Western Province Anglers' Union.)

CAPE TOWN TO CAPE HANGKLIP

Along the rocky coastline between Table Bay harbour and Hout Bay there are dense kelp beds, and hottentot is the most commonly caught species. During the winter months shoals of galjoen move into this area and are caught at places such as **Camps Bay, Boulders Beach** (near Bakoven) and **Llandudno**.

Between Hout Bay and Cape Point galjoen are caught in winter at such places as **Soetwater, Witsandbaai, Gifkommetjie, Pegrams Point, Neptunes Dairy** and **Pappies Bank**.

Hout Bay harbour has a marina where offshore tuna cruisers may be moored. There is also a slipway where the ski-boaters launch to fish the offshore tuna grounds from October through to May.

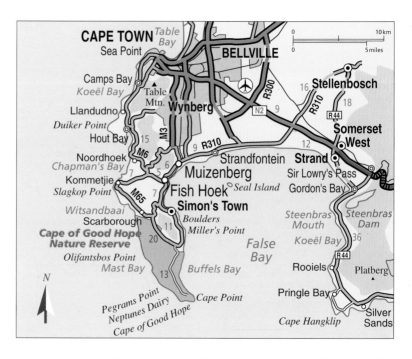

Apart from the beautiful scenery, the stretch of coastline from Cape Point to Cape Hangklip offers excellent fishing for both boat and shore anglers. Ski-boat anglers can launch their boats at **Buffels Bay** in the Cape Peninsula National Park, though numbers are limited by the local authority, and along the Simon's Town coastline at **Miller's Point**, and at the **Strand** and **Gordon's Bay**.

During the summer months small-boat anglers can catch kob, geelbek, shad and such bottomfish as red roman and red stumpnose close inshore from **Strandfontein** to the Strand. Yellowtail are also caught at places such as Muizenberg Corner, Seal Island and East Shoal, but the best yellowtail catches are made in the vicinity of **Cape Point**. The Bellows, Anvil Rock, South West Reef and Rocky Bank are the pinnacles and reefs where shoals of yellowtail are often found. Shore-based spinner fishermen catch yellowtail from ledges at

Rooikrans, Klein Rooikrans and Penguin Rock near Cape Point between October and April, while on the eastern side of False Bay yellowtail can be caught from the Rooiels ledges from February to April. In the summer months geelbek are occasionally caught close inshore between Cape Point and Rooikrans.

During the summer months beach anglers catch kob, shad and white steenbras along the stretch of coastline between **Muizenberg** and **Macassar**. White stumpnose are also caught (mostly at night) between September and November. From October through to April excellent catches of yellowfin and longfin tuna are made off Cape Point. Ski-boats launch at Miller's Point and fish for tuna up to 40 nautical miles offshore. Larger tuna cruisers leave from moorings at **Simon's Town** while a commercial line-fishing fleet operates out of **Kalk Bay**. Day charters can be arranged.

During the winter and spring months snoek shoals move into False Bay and good catches can be made anywhere between Miller's Point and Cape Point, or just off the point on South West Reef.

During the winter months surf anglers catch white steenbras and galjoen at places such as Strandfontein and Macassar, while rock anglers fish the rocky and dangerous coastline between Gordon's Bay and Cape Hangklip for species such as blacktail, *wildeperd* and galjoen.

At **Cape Hangklip** boat anglers fishing from tiny dinghies make excellent catches of geelbek at night in Maasbaai when the southeaster is blowing a gale.

HERMANUS TO CAPE AGULHAS

Hermanus was once the most popular and productive fishing resort along the Cape coastline but sadly this is no longer the case as catches are now generally poor. The lagoon at Hermanus offers safe angling to the small-boat enthusiast. Here catches of kob, shad, white steenbras and garrick are made during the summer months.

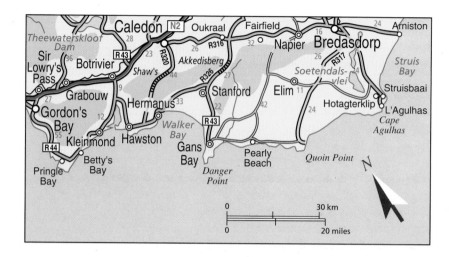

Die Plaat, a stretch of beach between Hermanus and Gansbaai still produces good catches of white steenbras and galjoen during the winter months.

A small fleet of purse-seiners operates out of the fisheries harbour at **Gansbaai** and sardine (pilchard), the most popular bait for kob and geelbek, are easily obtained here. Ski-boats launch at the launching ramp in the harbour and fish off **Danger Point** for bottomfish and pelagics such as yellowtail and geelbek.

The water along the stretch of coast between Danger Point and Cape Agulhas is very shallow and shore angling is largely dependent on the prevailing wind direction. Southerly and southeasterly winds blow onshore and produce the 'ginger beer' water in which excellent catches of kob are made at **Franskraal, Pearly Beach** and **Die Dam** and elsewhere. Good catches of galjoen and white steenbras are also made here during late winter and spring.

STRUISBAAI TO CAPE ST BLAIZE
This stretch of coastline probably offers the most productive fishing waters along the Cape coast. They cater for rock and surf, ski-boat and estuarine angling. Rivers such

as the Breede, Kafferkuils and Gourits are well known for their excellent catches of kob, while good catches of spotted grunter and white steenbras are also made.

The banks off **Agulhas, Struisbaai** and further up the coast at **Arniston** are regarded as the home of the yellowtail. Each year shoals of yellowtail appear during October and may be caught throughout the summer months until April. The best catches are made off Struisbaai and skiboats launch in the harbour, which becomes very busy at the height of the season. Good catches of kob and geelbek are also made from boats during the summer months. Bottomfish species are no longer as abundant as in earlier years, more than likely as a result of the large number of boats that gather here during the summer months.

White steenbras, shad, kob and garrick are caught from the shore (mainly along the beach) during the summer months, while galjoen are in the best possible condition during the late winter months.

On the stretch of coast between Cape Infanta and Witsand is the **Breede River**, the largest river flowing into the sea along the southern Cape coast. It is a particularly good spot for the estuarine angler as, apart from the large

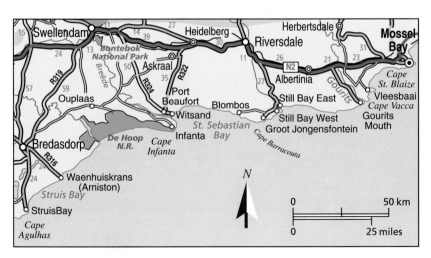

kob that are landed there each year, good catches of spotted grunter, white steenbras and garrick are also taken.

Experienced ski-boat anglers take their boats through the mouth of the Breede River to fish the bay for bottomfish such as *dageraad*, red stumpnose and santer. Kob fishing in the bay is good but the fish are normally smaller than those caught in the river.

Cape Infanta, west of the river mouth, has a slipway where ski-boats can be launched. The slip is steep and the launch can be quite eventful as the ramp faces the open sea and is situated among reefs. The shore fishing around Infanta is good as the water is deep and, apart from the panfish species, sought-after fish such as white musselcracker and poenskop are caught off the cliffs and ledges.

The Kafferkuils River divides the village of Still Bay into two separate resorts, **Still Bay East** and **Still Bay West**. The river, although much smaller than the Breede, is good for kob, spotted grunter, white steenbras and garrick. Offshore, excellent hauls of kob are made.

Shore anglers catch kob, shad and white musselcracker as well as smaller panfish during the summer months. Places such as Jongensfontein and Blombos are well known for the galjoen catches that are made there during the late winter months.

Gouritsmond is a holiday resort at the mouth of the Gourits River. It has a small hotel and is popular among anglers for its boat as well as rock and surf angling. From the shore some of the more sought-after species are caught, such as white musselcracker and poenskop, while the gully fishing for panfish is often very rewarding.

Small-boat anglers fish the Gourits River for kob, white steenbras, spotted grunter and garrick, while the more adventurous ski-boaters launch from the beach to fish for kob off the river mouth, or for bottomfish towards nearby **Kanon Point** or **Ystervarkfontein** 20 kilometres to the west.

Located 35 kilometres from Mossel Bay, **Vleesbaai** offers good surf angling along the beach, which stretches as far as Dana Bay to the east, while 5 kilometres away the **Fransmanshoek peninsula** is well known for the catches of kob, shad, garrick, white musselcracker and galjoen that have been made at places such as The Saddle, Tiergat, Malbaai and Fonteintjies. From The Saddle – a deep-water spot at the end of the headland – large sharks and other gamefish such as yellowtail have also been caught.

MOSSEL BAY TO CAPE ST FRANCIS

The coastline from Mossel Bay to Herolds Bay changes from a long stretch of beach to one of the southern Cape's most exposed sections of coastline. From October through to March anglers fishing off the rugged cliffs catch white musselcracker and poenskop along with shad and the common panfish species. Fishing off the cliffs can be dangerous and anglers are advised to be very careful, particularly when gaffing large fish on the lower ledges.

Mossel Bay has a launching ramp for ski-boats, situated close to the harbour. The ramp is safe to launch from in most weather conditions and provides access to good bay fishing for kob and garrick. In the past, good catches of gamefish such as yellowfin tuna, yellowtail and skipjack have been made further offshore. 'Couta, a warm-water species that normally occurs much closer to KwaZulu-Natal, has also been taken here.

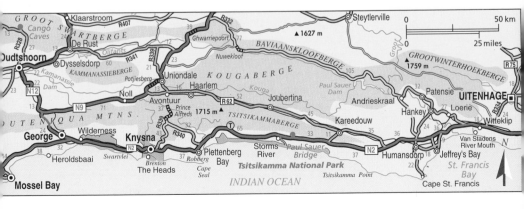

The town of **Knysna** has developed along the edge of the beautiful Knysna Lagoon, which offers light-tackle boat and shore anglers ideal conditions in which to pursue their sport. The moored boats of the residents and regular visitors are dotted along the edge of the lagoon, while boats on trailers can be launched at the ramp close to the railway bridge. Shallow-draft boats are necessary to fish the prawn flats and channels for species such as kob, spotted and white steenbras, Cape stumpnose and garrick. The safe fishing along the edge of the lagoon allows young anglers to hone their skills.

Bigger ski-boats need to stick to the deeper channels on their way to the open sea. The passage through the Knysna Heads can be dangerous and should not be attempted by inexperienced boat handlers or visitors who are unfamiliar with local conditions. The offshore fishing for reef fish is reasonable, while gamefishing for species such as yellowtail can be very inconsistent.

Shad and garrick are caught near The Heads from the shore, and kob, galjoen, white steenbras and blacktail are caught by rock and surf anglers fishing along the coastline from **Brenton-on-Sea** to the mouth of **Swartvlei Lagoon** in the Wilderness National Park.

Although heavily fished, **Plettenberg Bay** produces good catches throughout the year with the period October to April being the peak fishing season. In the bay white steenbras, kob and shad are caught from the beach and rocky ledges, while kob, spotted grunter, white steenbras and Cape stumpnose are caught by the estuarine anglers in the nearby Keurbooms and Bitou rivers.

Ski-boats are launched at Beacon Isle beach or through the mouth of the nearby Keurbooms River. Angling for garrick behind the beach-break in the bay and kob fishing off Keurboomsstrand are both beats of ski-boat anglers. Fishing on the bottom in deeper water can also produce good catches of hake.

The **Robberg peninsula** is famous for its spinner and

live-bait fishing for yellowtail and garrick. Yellowfin tuna move close to the shore when they appear in the bay and are taken by ski-boaters as well as anglers spinning from the ledges at Robberg. White musselcracker, shad, galjoen, blacktail and other panfish are also caught along Robberg at places such as Suidoos Bank, Voorstraat and Agterstraat.

Twenty-two kilometres from Humansdorp lies **Cape St Francis**, a popular holiday and fishing resort. Estuarine anglers catch kob, spotted grunter and garrick in the Krom River, while rock and surf anglers fish either off the headlands for white musselcracker and poenskop or the shallow bays for panfish, such as bronze bream, blacktail, wildeperd and galjoen. Shore gamefishermen fish the deep waters off spots such as Seal Point and Shark Point. Bronze whalers, along with gamefish such as yellowtail and garrick, provide good sport fishing. Large shad are also likely to take baits intended for gamefish.

Situated in St Francis Bay, **Jeffreys Bay** is probably better known as one of southern Africa's finest surfing spots. It is also popular among shell collectors who are attracted by the large variety of sea shells that wash ashore here.

Jeffreys Bay is the centre of a commercial squid fishery and the reefs are heavily fished by ski-boats and commercial line-fishing boats. As a result, reef fish are scarce although reasonable catches of kob can still be expected. Offshore, in the current, ski-boat anglers troll for yellowfin tuna in the summer when conditions are suitable.

PORT ELIZABETH TO PORT ALFRED
Shore fishing from the reefs and beaches to the west of **Port Elizabeth** is surprisingly productive. Good catches of kob and white steenbras are made off the beaches at places such as **Maitlands River Mouth** and **Van Stadens River Mouth**, while white musselcracker, bronze bream and galjoen are caught among the reefs.

Anglers fishing from small bay-boats in Algoa Bay are likely to catch shad, kob and garrick, while the bigger

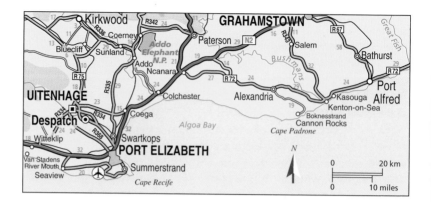

boats fish offshore for gamefish such as yellowfin tuna, skipjack and yellowtail. These boats also make good catches of hake when fishing on the bottom. Ski-boats launch from sites such as the ramp in the harbour, at **Sardinia Bay**, some 20 kilometres west of Port Elizabeth, or through the mouth of the Swartkops River.

The light-tackle boat angler will find that the coastline between Boknesstrand and East London is a particularly good area to visit. Rivers such as the Bushmans and Kariega are navigable for many kilometres upstream and rewarding to fish for the typical estuarine species: kob, spotted grunter, white steenbras and Cape stumpnose.

Ski-boats launch off the beach at **Cannon Rocks, Boknesstrand** and **Kenton-on-Sea** and often return with good catches of carpenter (silverfish) and the more common reef fish as well as kob and geelbek. Shore anglers in this area catch bronze bream, kob, musselcracker, shad and blacktail.

Port Alfred, mid-way between Port Elizabeth and East London, is one of the most popular eastern Cape holiday resorts. The Kowie River, which offers excellent estuarine angling for kob, garrick and spotted grunter, bisects the town and is a very busy waterway. Sport as well as commercial fishing boats are moored in the river or at small private jetties and the breakwater, which channels the mouth of the river and provides a reasonably safe passage to the open sea. Ski-boats fish the offshore reefs for kob, geelbek, red steenbras and carpenter.

THE GREAT FISH RIVER TO THE GREAT KEI RIVER

The **Great Fish River** demarcates the southern border of what was Ciskei and is a popular fishing spot for kob, white steenbras and spotted grunter. Rock and surf angling in the vicinity of the mouth also realises good catches of kob, white steenbras and other small panfish.

The holiday resort of **Hamburg** is situated on the bank of the Keiskamma River, near the mouth. The river is renowned for its excellent kob and spotted grunter fishing and is well worth visiting. Exceptionally large kob have been landed here by anglers fishing off small boats, mostly at night. Kob, shad, white steenbras and bronze bream constitute a large proportion of the catches made along the coastline on either side of the river mouth.

The commercial harbour at the mouth of the Buffalo River is the focal point of the city of **East London**. Not only of commercial importance, it also provides a safe passage to the offshore bottomfishing grounds for the local sport-fishing and commercial fleets. The offshore reefs are the prime angling area for such sought-after bottom species as poenskop and red steenbras. It is not uncommon for

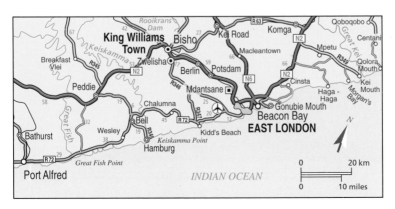

anglers to return from the offshore reefs with red steen-bras weighing up to 40 kilograms, and sometimes more.

Trolling at the current can produce a mixed bag of gamefish such as yellowfin tuna, dorado and skipjack, and sometimes marlin are found in the blue water. When conditions are favourable, the harbour wall itself is a good place to fish for kob, white steenbras, shad and garrick. Visiting anglers should note, however, that the west bank breakwater can be very dangerous when the sea is rough.

There are many places close to the city where shore anglers can fish for panfish (bronze bream, blacktail and, occasionally, white musselcracker and poenskop). German Bay, Nahoon Point and Hood Point are spots that are well worth visiting.

North of East London the sandy beaches are separated by rocky points or outcrops. Bronze bream, blacktail, kob and shad are the types of fish normally caught here. White musselcracker and garrick are caught where the water is deep close to the shore.

The Kei River, which forms the southern border of Transkei, offers estuarine fishing for the small-boat angler and a river launching area for ski-boaters wishing to fish the offshore reefs for kob and such sought-after bottomfish as poenskop and red steenbras. The little town of **Kei Mouth** is one of many picturesque holiday resorts that can be found along the stretch of coastline north of East London.

Ski-boat anglers should note that there is a marine reserve between the Nyara River mouth and the Great Kei mouth which extends 3 nautical miles seawards. Similar reserves closer to East London are those between Christmas Rock and the Gxula River mouth, and between Nahoon Point and Gonubie Point.

Shore anglers can expect to catch kob and shad during the period May to November, while bronze bream and smaller panfish are caught throughout the year.

THE GREAT KEI RIVER TO THE UMTAMVUNA RIVER (FORMER TRANSKEI)

One would expect that the rugged beauty of this region would attract many holidaymakers to the area but the general state of the roads leading to the coast, the long distances one has to travel between resorts and the type of accommodation offered at most of the seaside resorts tend to attract more anglers than tourists. Fishermen firmly believe that the rougher the road or the more remote the territory, the better the fishing will be!

The region's coastline is both scenic and dangerous. At many places the cliffs are steep and the water deep close to the sides. Here fishing can be hazardous, as large swells caused by south-westerly winds blowing against the current can appear out of the blue and sweep the unsuspecting angler off the rocks. Finding bait can also be difficult as the intertidal zone is heavily exploited and it is best to bring your own. If this is not possible certain types of bait can be purchased from the local people.

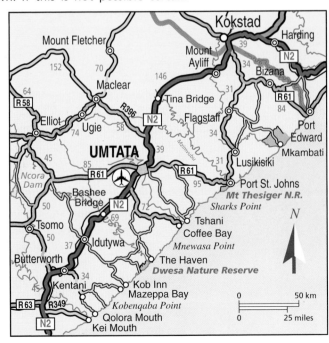

From Kentani to the sea, the road leads to the holiday homes at Kobenqaba and two hotel resorts, Seagulls and Trennerys, close to the mouth of the **Qolora River**.

Rock and surf anglers can expect to catch kob, shad and garrick, and panfish such as bronze bream, galjoen, blacktail, stonebream and *wildeperd* along this stretch of coastline. Further north the high rocks at **Kobenqaba**, once a well-known kite-angling spot, are well worth trying for white musselcracker and poenskop.

Throughout the years **Mazeppa Bay**, a popular fishing and holiday resort, has attracted anglers who concentrate on catching the larger gamefish such as yellowtail, garrick and various species of sharks from the shore. Where the water is deep these sought-after gamefish move in close to the shore and at popular places such as the Island and Shark Point the fish are well within reach of anglers casting their spinners or fishing with live baits. Kite fishing for sharks such as hammerheads adds to the excitement, and some spectacular catches have been made in the past.

Gully fishermen can expect to catch species such as bronze bream, *wildeperd*, blacktail, white steenbras and galjoen in this region.

Situated at the mouth of the Qora River, the **Kob Inn** resort is known as a hot spot for kob and white steenbras. The white steenbras arrive here on their migratory route from the Cape and excellent catches are made in and around the river mouth during the winter months. This is a particularly good spot for estuarine anglers who prefer to fish for kob and white steenbras with light tackle. Ski-boat anglers launch through the mouth of the river to fish the offshore reefs for bottomfish. Large red steenbras and poenskop are often landed here.

Coffee Bay shares the attraction of Mazeppa Bay as a holiday and fishing resort. Its sheltered beach offers safe bathing, while the shore and boat fishing can be excellent. Boats are launched at Coffee Bay or at Mapuzi Point just north of Coffee Bay. The offshore reefs are known for their good hauls of bottomfish, and large poenskop and large red steenbras are brought ashore here.

Panfish such as bronze bream, blacktail and galjoen (known as damba in this region) are caught along the rocky shoreline to the north, while the deeper water and rocky ledges to the south, although extremely dangerous to fish, are where garrick, poenskop and shad can be caught.

The town of **Port St Johns**, situated at the mouth of the Mzimvubu River, is a worthwhile place to visit, being both scenic and wonderfully diverse as a fishing resort. It offers good shore angling to those who are prepared to walk the distance or climb down the cliffs. However, some of the best kob, garrick and spotted grunter fishing can be had in the river itself. While there are many spots along the river bank where anglers can fish, the best way to fish is from a small boat and, as far as kob is concerned, at night.

The rocks and ledges on either side of the mouth are proven spots for kob, shad, garrick and spotted grunter. At some of the more remote spots poenskop can also be taken. Light-tackle gully anglers can fish the white water close to the rocks for bronze bream, galjoen and blacktail.

KWAZULU-NATAL

For rock and surf anglers, the KwaZulu-Natal south coast is a small paradise for several reasons. Firstly, the very broken coastline has produced many spots where the angler can stand high above the sea and cast into deep water. The numerous gullies and turbulent 'holes' that are a feature of much of the coastline are favourite spots for fish such as shad. Then there is the fact that the south coast can be regarded as a transition zone as it plays home to all of KwaZulu-Natal's warm-water fish species as well as many of the migratory Cape species.

For ski-boaters, the KwaZulu-Natal south coast is a favourite. A few easy surf launches (and some not so easy) put you into waters rich in gamefish such as 'couta, queen mackerel, wahoo and billfish such as marlin and sailfish. There are also some very desirable bottomfish, and for the more avid bottomfishermen, the continental shelf is only a few miles out in places.

The best time to fish this coast is during winter and spring when bait species such as karanteen and mullet arrive, to be followed by the larger fish species – geelbek and garrick among them. During this time 'couta are also attracted to this area to await, along with the fishermen and seine-netters, the arrival of the annual sardine run.

Some of the more popular south coast launching sites are at Umkomaas, Park Rynie, Hibberdene, Pumula, Shelly Beach and Ramsgate.

Although not as popular among holidaymakers as the south coast, the warm tropical conditions of the north coast attract anglers from all over southern Africa. The large variety of species as well as the opportunity to do battle with marlin and sailfish are drawcards that have made places such as Cape Vidal and Sodwana Bay the mecca of ski-boat gamefishing.

PORT EDWARD TO HIBBERDENE

Port Edward, close to the Eastern Cape border, affords some very productive fishing. Port Edward itself attracts shad in big shoals and there are a few places on the point

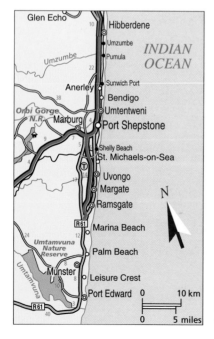

from which anglers can cast their offerings out to where the big gamefish roam. It is also a recognized ski-boat launch and puts ski-boat anglers in close proximity to some excellent bottomfishing, starting immediately behind the shark nets. Gamefish too swim close inshore and many a giant 'couta has been taken here. (Bear in mind that south of the launch to the Eastern Cape border is a marine reserve and no bottomfishing is allowed at a depth of less than 20 fathoms deep.)

A few kilometres north is **Glenmore** – a small bay known as a hot spot for kob, shad and shark, and more big 'couta have been taken from the famous Glenmore Pulpit Rock than from any other rock and surf spot in KwaZulu-Natal.

Towards Margate are numerous points producing good catches, as well as some long, flat beaches with scattered reefs in the surf zone that are good for bronze bream and kob.

Excellent catches of shad are made at Blue Bay, **Ramsgate**.

Attracting anglers from all over the country, the pier at **Margate** is a major facility, built specifically so that anglers can cast into deep water no matter whether it is high or low tide. This gives even the novice a good chance to hook a large kob, garrick or 'couta. Along the coast south of the pier are a few small scenic bays that offer productive fishing when the pier is too crowded.

To the north of the pier, Lucien is the start of a spate of productive spots for big fish, among them Pothole and Orange Rocks. Then comes **Uvongo,** where there is also a small pier from which anglers make excellent catches of shad. Poenskop are also caught here.

The next important stretch of coast is **Shelly Beach**, home to the famous launch site, Sonny Evans Small Craft Harbour. Hundreds of boats launch here, from where they head for the Protea Reef some 5 nautical miles offshore, right in the middle of the Agulhas current. Here a variety of gamefish can be caught, including 'couta, kingfish, yellowfin tuna and large yellowtail. By gentleman's agreement no bottomfishing is allowed, nor are anglers supposed to exploit the juvenile yellowfin tuna that feed here. These fish mature at around 35 kilograms and anything under 10 kilograms should be released.

The Umzimkulu River is sourced high in the Drakensberg, and by the time it reaches the ocean it is carrying plenty of water. **Port Shepstone**, lying at its mouth, was once a harbour for tugs and ocean-going ships but the erosion of the catchment areas has slowly reduced this once impressive river mouth to little more than a muddy water outlet. Nonetheless, there are still a few fish to be caught when the tide is high, and when some seawater moves into it the odd garrick is taken off the south wall.

The harbour continues to be used as a launch site but in winter it closes up so that making one's way through the surf can be hair-raising, even for an experienced skipper.

On the whole, the fishing in this area is good and the famous Sandspit – a long stretch of sand that is raised high above sea level – enables anglers to cast into a deep channel between the back-line and shore-break. It is almost always dirty water but the kob thrive in it and some outstanding catches are made both by novices and experienced anglers. At one end of the sandspit is Chaka's Rock, which is easy to fish and worthy of mention.

A feature of the point below the lighthouse is The Block – a big concrete pier from which anglers cast live baits into what must be garrick headquarters in KwaZulu-Natal. The stretch of water in front of the Port Shepstone lighthouse is a favourite place for garrick, and when the water clears somewhat in winter, spearfishermen report seeing hundreds of this species moving in and out of the backline. Other fish, such as white musselcracker and spotted grunter, also favour this area.

The next stop is **Umtentweni**, which has a reef that starts from the point and extends into progressively deeper water. This is another hot spot for bronze bream.

Sea Park point is the next rocky promontory. The little bay at its base is a favourite feeding ground for garrick and kob, and at **Sunwich Port**, a few kilometres north, is a huge rock, from which just a small cast will put you into productive calm water. **Pumula** is a launch site with a long expanse of beach that has a few reefs close to the shore which are good for bronze bream.

Umzumbe is home to Stebelle Rocks, a long point with a bay on the south side. Both 'couta and queen mackerel frequent this area and are taken off the rocks. Shad too move into the bay in large numbers.

HIBBERDENE TO DURBAN

This section of the south coast offers some good launch sites. Launching at **Hibberdene** puts ski-boaters out into some of the most productive waters along this stretch of coast, especially those at Mfazazana a few kilometres to the north. The quiet little village of **Mtwalume** also provides boat launching facilities and has a number of excellent fishing spots close by.

Further north is Umdoni Point at **Pennington** where good catches of shad, kingfish, kob and gamefish are made. Close by is Happy Wanderers (**Kelso**), another typical point and long beach with a deep channel running through in front of the back-line.

Next comes **Rocky Bay** with a good launch site and, for shore anglers, another large concrete structure built on the shore line at the base of the point, from which bait can be cast into productive waters. Galjoen, shad and bronze bream frequently move into the bay here, although it is a bit overfished.

Umkomaas is very similar to Umzimkulu geographically and, again, good fishing is to be had here. It is a known hot spot for 'couta, kob and giant kingfish. It is also a launch site that services anglers and divers wishing to venture out to the Aliwal Shoal.

Winkelspruit, Warner Beach, Amanzimtoti and, just before Durban, **Isipingo** are more fishing spots worth visiting, though the choice will depend on prevailing conditions. Isipingo is very sheltered and has interesting reefs which attract shad. It is also a launch site and puts ski-boaters within reach of some outstanding reefs about 10 nautical miles offshore. Poenskop, kob and geelbek are taken in big numbers in these areas.

Despite the heavy fishing pressure from local as well as visiting anglers, the beaches and groynes close to the city of **Durban**, as well as North Pier and South Pier, are worth fishing, especially if you keep a close eye on the weather and sea conditions.

On the beaches anglers fishing with baitfish can catch kob, shad, sharks (mainly dusky) and

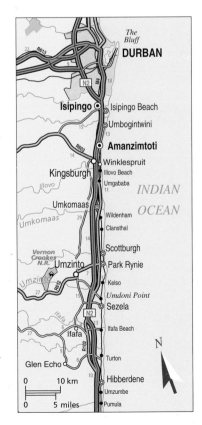

rays. Other species like Natal stumpnose, spotted grunter and pompano may be caught on mole crab, cracker shrimp and mussels close to the sandbanks.

The harbour is an easily accessible and popular fishing spot. Shad, kob, spotted grunter and Natal stumpnose can be taken from the northern breakwater. The southern breakwater, although dangerous at times, is one of the most popular local fishing spots. Through the years excellent catches of gamefish and large sharks have been made here and although the action is not as fast and furious as in previous years, 'couta and queen mackerel, geelbek and sharks are still caught by experienced anglers who know the best conditions in which to fish for these species.

Offshore boats launch at Durban Ski-boat Club or leave from moorings in the harbour to fish the bay and further offshore for 'couta, yellowfin tuna, prodigal son, wahoo, sailfish and marlin.

UMHLANGA ROCKS TO KOSI BAY

From **Umhlanga Rocks to Mtunzini** much the same species are caught from the shore. During the winter months shad, kob and garrick are the more common species caught, while the summer bag of panfish may include pompano and Natal stumpnose. Sand sharks provide the best sportfishing and skates and rays, by virtue of their mass, test an angler's powers of endurance.

This area is far more densely populated than the rest of the north coast and the resorts are closer together. Ski-boats are launched at most of the resorts to fish for pelagic gamefish species as well as for billfish such as marlin and sailfish.

The harbour at **Richard's Bay,** which is well known as a coal-loading terminal, is also popular with ski-boat anglers. In the harbour, boat anglers can fish for kob, shad, garrick and grunter, while the launch in the shelter of the harbour also offers easy access to the nearby gamefishing grounds. Wahoo, kingfish, 'couta and yellowfin tuna are the predominant species in this area.

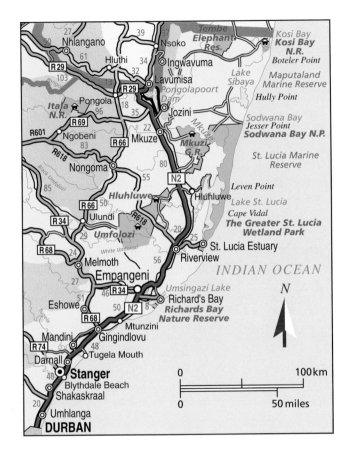

Shore angling along this coastal stretch is also productive and yields good catches of giant kingfish, Natal stumpnose, spotted grunter, white steenbras, pompano and sharks.

St Lucia is a holiday resort which is especially geared to cater for the needs of visiting anglers. The lake offers excellent light-tackle fishing from small boats or the shore. Ski-boats launch in the estuary to fish places such as the lighthouse, or northwards as far as **Cape Vidal**, for such gamefish as wahoo, 'couta, queenfish, marlin and sailfish.

Estuary fishing from small boats for kob, spotted grunter and shad is a favourite pastime. The annual grunter run,

which happens between August and November, is a special event and attracts many boat and shore anglers.

In a paradise of vast, unspoilt beaches, which is one of the rewards of fishing at St Lucia, surf anglers are likely to catch shad, spotted grunter, kob, sharks and rays.

Nearby **Cape Vidal** shares Sodwana Bay's attraction as a north-coast gamefishing hot spot. For the shore angler, the rocky ledges to the south of the bay are an excellent place to fish for gamefish and produce good catches of giant kingfish, queenfish and various species of sharks.

Sodwana Bay is one of the billfish hot spots and very popular among ski-boaters. Blue, black and striped marlin as well as sailfish are caught here by gamefishermen who are prepared to live the bush-camp/game-fishing life that Sodwana is all about. Anglers fishing the beaches around Sodwana can expect to catch kingfish, queenfish, kob, shad, stumpnose and pompano.

The coastline between Cape Vidal and Kosi Bay is a marine reserve but, with the exception of two areas set apart as sanctuaries, angling (but not bait collecting) from the shore is permitted. At **Kosi Bay** anglers may fish only at Kosi Mouth and Banga Nek. Both these spots are good for gamefish such as giant kingfish and sharks. For the determined angler, Blackrock to the south is another spot that produces gamefish and large sharks.

As a resort **Kosi Bay** caters for shore as well as small-boat estuarine angling. However, due to the low salinity of Lake Nhlanga (the third lake in the Kosi system) anglers tend to concentrate on bottomfishing in the first two lakes where such species as spotted grunter, Natal stumpnose and river snapper can be caught throughout the year, although spring and autumn yield the best catches. Gamefish such as springer and barracuda are regularly caught, especially during the summer months.

APPENDIX I

THE TAG-AND-RELEASE PROGRAMME

Biological information and scientific analysis of catch records reveal that catches of most of our popular angling fishes are indeed declining. Whereas the reasons for such declines are not always immediately apparent, it nevertheless gives cause for concern. A number of research programmes have been launched throughout South Africa to investigate these trends and much valuable scientific information has been collected. For instance, we know that a female kob must be four years old before she spawns, that slinger change their sex from female to male at a size of 35 cm and that elf spawn in Natal. But we don't know which of our fish undertake migrations, which are locally resident, and at what rate most of our fishes grow. The finest way to obtain such data is through a large-scale tagging programme. But there are too few marine biologists available to do the actual tagging, therefore the obvious solution lies with the involvement of the angling public, where large-scale angler participation can ensure adequate numbers of fish tagged and released.

WHO SHOULD TAG? It is already common practice for sport fishermen to release their catch unharmed. If you are one of these then tagging may well provide you with an additional interest in your favourite sport. Even if you do not normally release your fish, the skill and thrill of catching, tagging and releasing a fish unharmed is an experience not to be missed. Besides this, you will be making a valuable contribution to the research and future wellbeing of your own sport. Once you have tagged a fish you retain your stake in the research programme because, in the event of it being recaught, you will receive notification of your fish's growth, migration and recapture.

To ensure success in this programme it will be necessary to recruit thousands of anglers of all types. If you are a keen angler with the long-term interest of your sport at heart why not participate in this joint nationwide tagging venture?

TAGGING PROCEDURES Obviously some species are more desirable to tag than others. If only sharks and barbel were to be tagged the programme would not reach its full potential. In essence the more cherished your catch, the greater also is its tagging value. Anglers are not expected, of course, to release all their prize landings, but if anglers tagged one in five of their catch, the resultant scientific contribution would be massive. (As the tags themselves are expensive, there is a considerable onus on the angler not to misplace them and to return any unused tags.)

Detailed instructions are provided with each tagging kit, which comprises an applicator with ten tags, brochures, tagging stickers, etc. – all in a durable container. As the programme grows new types of tags will be developed for specific tasks. The tagging of stingrays, for instance, has not yet been undertaken but it will not be long before equipment will be available for this purpose. The tagging itself is not a difficult procedure, but it does require gentle handling of the fish and care with the equipment.

Anglers who subscribe to the programme will receive regular newsletters with updated information on the latest taggings and recaptures. Their own recaptures will also be acknowledged with a computer analysis of the fish's migration details.

FISH CURRENTLY TARGETED INCLUDE garrick, kob, galjoen, yellowtail, geelbek, spotted grunter, 'couta (king mackerel), musselcracker, white steenbras, kingfish, poenskop and red stumpnose.

HOW TO JOIN This tagging programme has to be run along fairly formal lines so that the research and administration can function smoothly. There is a minimum donation of R65, not only to offset some of the costs but also to ensure that the angler will be more seriously committed to the project. Once an angler has joined, his or her name, address and other details will be captured onto the Oceanographic Research Institute (ORI)'s computers and the applicant will receive all further correspondence and notification. For details, write to: THE TAGGING OFFICER, P. O. BOX 736, DURBAN 4000.

REFERENCES

BIDEN, C.L. *Sea-Angling Fishes of the Cape* (third edition). Cape Town, Juta & Co., 1954.

BRANCH, M. & G. *The Living Shores of Southern Africa*. Cape Town, C. Struik, 1981.

COMPAGNA, L.J.V., EVERTS, D.A. & SMALE, M.J. *Guide to the Sharks and Rays of Southern Africa*. Cape Town, Struik Publishers, 1989.

DAY, J.H. *A Guide to Marine Life on South African Shores*. Cape Town, A.A. Balkema, 1969.

GOODBY, P. *Big Fish and Blue Water*. Sydney, Angus & Robatson, 1970.

HOME, C. *Saltwater Fishing in South Africa*. Cape Town, Howard Timmins, 1961.

HOME, C. *Game Fishing Transformed*. Cape Town, Don Nelson, 1974.

HOME, C. *Fisherman's Eldorado*. Cape Town, Howard Timmins, 1955.

HORROBIN, P., man. ed. *Gregory's Fishing Guide*. (12th edition). New South Wales, Australia, Gregory's Publishing Co., 1991.

JONES, L. *Angler's Atlas: Durban to Sodwana*. Durban, Len Jones Fishing Guide, 1981.

LILLIECROMA, K.T. *Salt-water Fish and Fishing in Southern Africa*. Johannesburg, Nelson, 1966.

PAYNE, A.I.L. & CRAWFORD, J.M. eds. *Oceans of Life*. Cape Town, Vlaeberg Publishers, 1989.

SCHOEMAN, S. *Strike!* (2nd edition). Cape Town, A.A. Balkema, 1962.

SMITH, M.M. & HEEMSTRA, P.C, eds. *Smith's Sea Fishes*. Johannesburg, MacMillan, 1986.

South African Road Atlas (9th edition). Cape Town, Map Studio.

TAYLOR, V. *Sedgwick's Old Brown Rock and Surf Angling Guide: Southern Coast*. Cape Town, Stellenbosch Farmer's Winery.

VAN DEN BERG, A. *Angling in False Bay*. Cape Town, Timmins Publishers, 1984.

VAN DER ELST, R.P. *A Guide to the Common Sea Fishes of Southern Africa*. Cape Town, C. Struik, 1981.

WHIBLEY, I. & GARATT, P. *The South African Fisherman*. Cape Town, Struik Timmins, 1989.

Catch Restrictions, Marine Reserves and Restricted Areas

For the latest information on the above, contact:

MARINE AND COASTAL MANAGEMENT
Private Bag x2
Roggebaai
8012
Tel: (021) 402 3911

INDEX